IN SEARCH OF MORE EFFECTIVE SERVICE:

Inquiry as a Guiding Image for Educational Reform in America

Hendrik D. Gideonse

༚

In the late 1960's before our sons were born
when Sarah and I worked together
for U.S.O.E.'s research programs
we would be asked regularly if we had any children.
In the hubris of youth I used to respond,
"No.....just 50,000,000 American ones!"
It is to them -- plus two -- and the rising generations
behind them to whom this essay is dedicated.

- H.D.G.

EXECUTIVE SUMMARY

The rightful place of American education on the national agenda has been restored. Numerous reports and studies, released and forthcoming, afford ample evidence of the depth of concern and the willingness to expend energy in the search for solutions to identified needs. Too much of the discussion about education reform to date, however, has dwelt on symptoms. Far too many simplistic solutions have been advanced. Despite the clear dismay expressed over teacher quality, little has been said about teacher education. Even less has been said about what actually goes on in instructional settings and the basic assumptions actually guiding the conduct of professional practice in schooling. Few of the analyses have recognized the complexity of current circumstance; the result has been an essential fragmentation of proposed treatments.

America's educational systems must find their reformation but not through piecemeal attempts. Current problems are caused by many factors but one crucial element is flawed assumptions about teaching, learning, and the requirements of truly professional practice. The solution lies in a more fundamental reconstruction based on new assumptions more likely to take us past our present problems to higher horizons of effective performance.

Existing Assumptions Underlying Instruction

American schooling rests on three assumptions. As a Nation we have been willing to rely on the intrinsic satisfaction of working with young people as the prime motivator for the professionals. Teaching is seen as the transmission of content. The route to teacher preparation is academic training, a very modest "internship" experience, and the accumulation of individual, personal experience. These three assumptions mean that we have basically approached teaching as if it were a performing art rather than a true profession.

Inquiry as an Organizing Principle for Teaching

A fundamental rethinking of the basic assumptions guiding the Nation's schools, colleges and universities in carrying out their instructional responsibilities is now possible and required if the advances now being demanded by the public and its elected representatives are to be achieved. New assumptions must be adopted. The new assumptions proposed for consideration are:

1. Professional educators ought always to act on knowledge about teaching and learning.

2. Systematic and reflective inquiry ought to become the underlying professional frame of mind that guides teachers, administrators, teacher educators, and policy

officials in the daily conduct of their responsibilities.

3. The products of inquiry required for more effective service are practical and immediate as well as theoretical and conceptual. They include the rationales connecting recommended courses of action to intended outcomes as well as the invention of techniques, materials, and prescriptions designed to achieve those outcomes.

Rigorous commitment to either the knowledge base or inquiry practices in support of instruction does not now characterize professional preparation programs or the operation of the Nation's schools and colleges. The miniscule nature of the research and development sector for education offers further evidence of the weakness of the commitment of the Nation to grounding educational practice on knowledge and inquiry. Furthermore, the stifling isolation of practitioners from one another in the performance of their professional duties reduces dramatically the opportunity for productive practical inquiry supportive of improvements in service.

The proposed change in basic assumptions orients the profession to that which can be **warranted as known**, that is, what can be justified by theoretical and practical knowledge, valid argument, sound judgment, and continuous inquiry processes.

Current Impediments

Seeking to ground the profession on the organizing principle of the processes and products of inquiry may seem unexceptional. Yet our educating institutions are not now so organized. Furthermore, attempts to move in this direction over the past two decades have been less than dramatic in their effect. The reasons are many.

They include:

° Incomplete -- and sometimes erroneous -- conceptions of how research and knowledge relate to practice improvement.

° Imperfect understandings of the characteristics of inquiry in support of education.

° The organization of schools which assumes neither the need for inquiry to guide practice nor a developing knowledge base to which practitioners require continuous exposure.

° The low status of the profession which has made attending to its knowledge base of dramatically lesser importance nationally.

° Understandably human reactions to the demands for change that developments in knowledge imply, reactions whose bases range from nostalgia for the past and complacency in the present situation, to fear of the implications of change.

° Genuine doubts that the puzzles of educational practice will yield to the tools and products of inquiry.

Projected Outcomes of Organizing Education on Inquiry

Projected over three or four decades the outcomes of grounding education on the organizing principle of inquiry would be:

1. More effective schooling. Educators' actions will rest on what they need to know. They will be using systematic inquiry strategies to adjust practice to the requirements of emerging circumstances.

2. Educators' better relation to diverse stakeholder groups and individuals. Awareness of the contributions of behavioral and social inquiry will lead to a deeper appreciation of multiple perspectives and their importance to effective instructional practice.

3. Increased professional capacity of educators. Rigor will be demanded by the knowledge base. Teaching itself will become a more intellectually demanding and satisfying professional role because of its inquiry oriented character. This shift will attract and retain more capable individuals and stimulate higher performance from all.

4. Job differentiation within teaching. Hierarchically structured teaching teams will be responsible for groups of children in approximately the present teacher/student ratios. Multiple perspectives will thus be brought to bear on the practical problems of schooling, greater pooling of professional resources on the problems of instruction relative to enhancing student achievement will occur, and career paths **within** teaching will be created.

5. Teacher education becoming a post-baccalaureate enterprise. Teaching candidates will be admitted with a liberal arts degree having already mastered the content area they intend to teach. The number of institutions approved for offering professional preparation programs will decline by some 60 to 70 percent.

6. Greater unity, especially as between practitioners and teacher preparation programs, to a profession now not well integrated among its several parts.

7. Greatly increased resources for education's research and development sector.

8. Achieved at approximately a ten percent additional investment measured on current expenditure patterns. (The ten percent estimate does **not** include the resources now required to establish

a satisfactory base salary for teachers, especially at entry).

Examples, Purposes, and Characteristics of Educational Inquiry

To rest the educational system on knowledge and inquiry requires clarity respecting the nature of inquiry processes and products for education.

Examples of educational inquiry range from the research conducted to improve fundamental theory, to the design and development of learning-effective curricular materials, to the kinds of practical inquiry represented by attempts to secure information helpful in understanding the nature of a learning difficulty in a specific child.

The purposes of educational inquiry range from the development of theory to the formulation of policy, from inquiry conducted in instructional settings by teachers aimed at supporting the countless decisions and instructional design puzzles they face daily to practical inquiry in **support** of the instructional act (for example, that pertaining to the design and development of professional training programs). Educational development, the equivalent of the engineering function whereby sound theory is translated into materials, techniques and organizational design structures for schooling, is also important yet at present hardly supported.

Educational inquiry constitutes a substantial subset of the larger domain of behavioral and social inquiry. A proposal to ground the profession on the processes and products of inquiry needs to be understood in the context of its special characteristics. These include:

1. The almost limitless number of variables and the great difficulty in controlling them for purposes of study or practical effect.

2. The great complexity of the relationships among the variables including the extent to which the effects of variables acting on one another may be simultaneous.

3. The metaphorical character of the terminology employed in educational inquiry. Meaning is often indirect or oblique and is inevitably invested with affective content.

4. The inescapability of value considerations. The concepts, methods, and modes of presentation of inquiry are inextricably bound up in values of many different kinds.

5. The influence of human consciousness. Mere attention to a topic subtly changes it, especially over time.

The effects of these five characteristics combine to yield three important second-order characteristics:

1. Behavioral and social inquiry will not have the cumulative character of research in the natural or bio-medical sciences.

It can, however, illuminate the current scene and generate data on which responsible action may be taken.

2. Because of the many variables and their complex interaction, the search for generalization, except as it is oriented to theoretical understanding, may well be over-emphasized. The need for inquiry strategies appropriate to specific sites and circumstances emerges as especially crucial.

3. Different kinds of people engaged in education know things in different, but not necessarily intellectually superior, ways. Academics' understandings or knowledge is of one kind, practitioners' of a second, and clients' and stakeholders' of still a third. Understanding the equal legitimacy but fundamental differences of these several ways of knowing is especially important for a proposed grounding of the profession of education on the processes and products of inquiry.

One of the major contributions of inquiry to educational practice is the recognition of the usefulness and the ubiquitousness of multiple perspectives of social reality. So, too, there are many views of how the work of the research and development sectors for education can have beneficial impact on educational practice. Those views constitute one of the frames of reference of performers of inquiry and indicate some of the values with which those performers are in alliance. Some views focus on the primacy of conceptual knowledge, some on the primacy of practical. Some look to the importance of the many participants in education and richness of their interactions as a community. Others focus on the role of individuals in innovation or on the crucial brokerage and linkage functions between researchers and practitioners. All may be appropriate, given different premises and circumstances.

Action Steps

Formulating an idea, exploring its implications, and projecting the consequences of acting on it over time is not an action plan. The second part of the essay consists of fifteen memoranda to sixteen role players in the larger educational policy and practice arenas. The sixteen roles do not exhaust the cast of characters, but those addressed cover the waterfront. While the suggestions and implications sketched for each are not exhaustive, actions appropriate to each role player are considered.

Teachers and principals are urged to examine their current roles for the inquiry activities they now carry out or might come to perform, and to seek support in their current settings for undertaking such activities to improve their present accomplishments. Governors should continue to lead in efforts to reform education. They should keep the pressure on educators and use their good offices to stimulate the coordinate attention of lower and higher education in their States. Chief State School Officers are urged to exercise the full potential of their leadership role in the development of a more unified profession.

Congress should address and meet the resource requirements of educational research and development now so drastically undersupported. Professional associations can help develop research agendas, stimulate an inquiry orientation among their practitioners, and work together in the interest of grounding professional practice on knowledge. Education writers in the popular press are urged to consider their own inquiry. Improvement of the quality of their reporting and analysis would diminish the extent to which their own present amateurism reflects unfairly on education.

College and university presidents must address inquiry processes on their own campuses relating to instruction, the resources that should be allocated for teacher preparation programs, and the crucial and presently badly under-served role of higher education to equip teachers with an effective liberal education. State boards of education must challenge the organized profession to live up to the public's expectations and to exercise teachers' developing powers and autonomy for constructive, responsible, and accountable ends.

The memorandum device, however, is more than a way of indicating what specific actions need to be taken. It also seeks to illustrate how effective reform, no matter what its organizing principles, will not be achieved without the coordinate and cooperative actions of a vast army of professionals and policy-makers.

The implications of grounding education on inquiry are extensive but manageable in the several decade time frame proposed. Sweeping change is called for, however, given the demands on education created by the sophistication of modern technology, the shrinking nature of the globe, and the need to preserve and perpetually reinvent the human and democratic principles undergirding the republic.

TABLE OF CONTENTS

Part Two

THE USES, PURPOSES, AND CHARACTERISTICS OF INQUIRY FOR EDUCATION

Part Three

FROM CONCEPT TO ACTION
(or, THEORY TO PRACTICE!)

Part Four

RESTATEMENT AND REJOINDERS

FOREWORD

How this essay came to be written has much to do with the career path of its author. Professor Richard Fenno, then at Amherst College, first exposed me to the concept of means/ends analysis. That exposure probably constituted my first explicit glimmer of what the study of policy might be about. Following graduate study in the foundations of education and a fascinating year as the entire education department at a small New England liberal arts college I was appointed Coordinator of the Social Sciences Curriculum Improvement Program of the U.S. Office of Education in 1964. A few months later, in July, 1965, I was invited to take the post of Director of Planning and Evaluation for the newly-organized Bureau of Research. Such an office had not existed before then; any achievements during the next six years were the result of help and encouragement received from many people in the research and larger educational policy communities, but they were also an outgrowth of whatever capacity my staff and I had to learn about and adapt to the constraints and opportunities of the Washington environment.

During my time as chief of research planning and evaluation for U.S.O.E. an opportunity presented itself to initiate and then undertake a major policy review of American education research and development. The review was conducted under the auspices of the Paris-based Organisation for Economic Co-operation and Development, a twenty-four member international organization committed to economic growth and employment, rising standards of living, and the expansion of world trade. Educational policy in support of economic growth and development had long been a key instrumental concern of O.E.C.D. In the sixties the directed search internationally for instructional and organizational improvement in education made O.E.C.D. responsive to a proposal that a so-called country review of educational policy be conducted focusing on educational research and development and using the United States as the vehicle. The review was conducted in 1969; my role, among other duties, included preparation of the national self study which formed the basis for examination by a four-member visiting team. Later, I served as one of the American delegates at the "confrontation session" at O.E.C.D. headquarters in Paris. The self-study was published in 1970 under the title Educational Research and Development in the United States.

In 1971 I joined the staff of Senator Abraham Ribicoff's Subcommittee on Executive Reorganization and Government Research. That was the year legislation creating the National Institute of Education was under Congressional consideration. I was able to play an active role in the analysis of issues and options respecting the proposed NIE.

The next year I assumed the deanship of the College of Education at the University of Cincinnati. My involvement in research policy issues continued. In 1977, for example, I was asked to serve as a member of the Congressionally-mandated panel to review the plans and operations of the regional educational laboratories and research and development centers, an assignment that lasted for more than two years. The panel's accomplishments contributed to improvement of the management and policy direction of the Lab/Center program administered by the National Institute of Education.

August, 1979, marked the beginning of an involvement in still another related activity. A dozen education deans, concerned to exercise greater and more effective leadership in the larger profession, convened over a period of eighteen months to consider how more systematic advance might be secured for education. Toward the end of our discussions, we prepared a draft policy statement advocating the central role of inquiry and scholarship in the teacher education domain and analyzing the implications of the position we espoused.[1] The statement was distributed to all heads of teacher education in America and to the presidents of the colleges and universities housing teacher education programs. Each recipient was offered a chance to respond to the propositions contained in the policy document. The experience of working on and following up the initiative taken by the group (whose members came to be called the Salishan Deans after the location of the conference site where we first began to work with one another) contributed to the impetus to undertake this present analysis.

The essay is directed to the policy community, the lay public, educational practitioners, and, lastly, the research community. Notes that may be of interest to professionals, scholars, or the policy research community have been indicated in superscript throughout the text, but placed at the end of the volume where they are less likely to interfere with the flow of the argument.

This effort has been an intensely personal one. I would be less than candid if I didn't admit that the dimensions of the task occasionally gave me great feelings of uneasiness. Part of the anxiety arose from the recognition that its very theme implied further development ought to be collaborative rather than individual. I wrestled with that implication and finally opted to present the ideas as an individual. Doing so does increase the chances of incompleteness and error. The reasons for taking that risk are several.

The first is very practical. The time available to me given my other roles as Dean, Professor, and (this year) President of the Association of Colleges and Schools of Education in State Universities and Land Grant Colleges was extremely limited. The development of the outline extended over the spring, but the initial draft was completed within the month of August when I was able to take time from my administrative duties.

Second, the policy discussion nationally about the state of education and what to do about it is taking place **now**; a potential contribution to that dialogue would have to appear quickly.

Third, the manner in which educational policy is formulated in America depends heavily on debate and discussion. We fully appreciate education's political ramifications and subject new ideas to intensive scrutiny. Our tradition, however, has tended to be "oral" meaning that ideas that are hastily formulated or merely a glimmer in the eye of an initial beholder are frequently lost or passed over. The present effort takes a single idea and develops it more fully and thoroughly. It is offered as a policy proposition, an hypothesis for others to react to, as a stimulus to further inquiry and response. In that sense it can be considered a piece of action policy research.

Many of my colleagues have offered encouragement and counsel. Without the support of people like Richard Wisniewski, David Krathwohl, Matthew Miles, Maxine Greene, Tom Green, John Egermeier, Carolyn Breedlove, Susan Opper, Elliot Eisner, Robert Koff, Nancy Bordier, Jeffrey Shultz, Leslie Salmon-Cox, Ed Meade, Ellis Joseph, Charles Case, David Imig, and Sarah Gideonse I might not have been emboldened to carry the project forward to completion. The stimulus provided by the re-reading of several excellent student papers on related topics, copies of which I have kept over the years, also should be acknowledged.[2] In addition to some of those already mentioned above, Lewis Jones, Glenn Markle, Robert Leestma, Nancy Hamant, Bob Yinger, G. David Schiering, Tom Lasley, Joel Milgram, William Nester, Norma Nutter, and Bill Russell counseled me on the draft. I hope I have left no one unmentioned who helped me better to present the ideas in this essay; if I have, herewith my apologies and thanks.

It also needs to be firmly stated that the work of many others whose names are liberally sprinkled through the notes has figured powerfully in my own thinking. George Herbert Mead taught that mind is a social phenomenon; the proposals formulated here would have been impossible without dependence on the ideas and analyses of countless others. My sons, Hendrik and Ted, didn't see quite as much of their Dad as they wanted the last two months, but they were willing to accept the explanation that their children might just be the beneficiaries of the time I withheld from them. To Sarah a special acknowledgement, familiar in one sense, but unusual in another. Her own near-completion of doctoral work in related social science fields provided renewed intellectual stimulus for us both, thus further enriching a partnership already appreciated for the extent to which it has, among other things, enabled me to make commitments whose completion measurably contributed to the development of the ideas contained herein.

Finally, deep thanks go to the Executive Board of the National Alumni Association of the College of Education at the University of Cincinnati for committing nearly half their small treasury to share equally with the College the printing costs of the essay. Equally deep appreciation exists for my colleagues, Dean Ellis Joseph of the College of Education, University of Dayton, Dean Richard Wisniewski of the College of Education at the University of Tennessee, and David Imig, Executive Director of the American Association of Colleges for Teacher Education, who severally agreed to help in meeting the costs of distribution of the essay to the educational policy community.

Cincinnati, Ohio
October, 1983

INTRODUCTION

Education once again occupies a prime spot on the national agenda. No single event, of course, ended the brief period of deliberate in- and under-attention of the first years of the Reagan administration. Still, the report of The National Commission on Excellence in Education[1] may be credited with focusing the national spotlight on persistent concerns about education resident throughout the Nation. While honest differences of opinion may exist over whether those concerns are properly or in what degree a matter for Federal attention, it is readily apparent now that the scope of the problem is national and multifaceted as is the energy to address it.

The report of the Excellence Commission was followed in short order by a number of others; it will be supplemented and complemented by still more in the months ahead.[2] The policy discussion spawned by the refocused national attention has addressed merit pay, master teachers, and the need for (or, conversely, the futility of) massive infusions of new money. It has considered the substantive and higher qualifications of teachers, the desirability of encouraging alternatives to public education through such proposals as tuition tax credits, and even somewhat incongrously stimulated a brief resurgence of Presidential attention to school prayer! The debate has also been confused, if not marred, by more narrow partisan concerns. The 1984 presidential candidates on the Democrat side have sought to capitalize on the depth of the renewed public concern that exists, and President Reagan further exacerbated his longstanding squabble with the National Education Association whose vigorous support of former President Carter and democratic candidates generally had earned Reagan's enmity.

Still, the resurgence of attention has been gratifying. Unless the focus of that attention becomes much more substantial and analytically sound,[3] however, not much of lasting value or significance is likely to emerge. The policy debate so far has been pretty thin gruel, indeed. The temptation is virtually irresistible to remind oneself of Mencken's bromide that for every complex social problem there is a simple, obvious solution that is wrong.

PROBLEMS

The problems the public and the policy sector see may be stated rather simply. The public finds the accomplishments of the educational system dissatisfying. It is deeply concerned about the present and future quality of the teaching staff. Parents and others required to relate to teachers and school administrators far too often find them bureaucratic and "system main-taining" in their orientation rather than overtly committed to achieving the ultimate purposes of schooling -- an educated, socially responsible citizenry, capable of coping with a complex technological (and shrinking) world, contributing through a capacity for employment in the world of work to their own and others' well-being. The public perceives present costs to be high, at least in terms of the quality of the benefits received. Consider a last indicator, in some respects the most poignant of all. What does the 1983 plethora of reports and analyses about education and educational policy tell us about the enterprise they purport to study? The answer is not just the obvious one, that so much is perceived to be wrong. It is also a non-obvious one: the flood occurs because the system itself is non-reflective, non-self-correcting, and apparently susceptible only to sporadic attempts from outside to "set things straight."

These deficiencies, however, are symptoms. The **real** problems are the root causes of that which dissatisfies us. Until these roots are accurately identified, successful treatment will elude us. Surely, no one in or out of education, set about devising a system with the shortcomings that now plainly exist. There must be good reasons why it is the way it is. And there are!

ROOT CAUSES

A listing of the reasons would include at least the following:

§ Goal Conflict - In his latest book A Place Called School John Goodlad illustrates the consequences of disagreement over goals when he notes the diversity of views of what schools ought to be for and the resulting certainty that serving any of those goals **too much** will generate dissatisfaction.[4]

§ Low Status - Teaching is a low status occupation and societal function. Advice flows from virtually every sector, rigor in its formulation or presentation is rarely demanded, and quality people (save, it would sometimes seem, the slightly crazy or the professional masochist) are discouraged from making it a career.

§ Low Income Incentives - The low status of the profession translates directly into low-level financial incentives for entering and remaining in the profession. Beginning police officers can earn twice the salary now of beginning teachers, for example, and the only method of salary advance in teaching is through earned academic credits (which may or may not improve capabilities or performance) or length of time on the job.[5]

§ "Union Control" - The heading is flanked by quotation marks because the root problem is more an abdication of public and administrative responsibility than misplaced control by the organized profession **per se**. Still, certain of the provisions that have been written into contracts with teachers or (just as significantly but more elusive) the practices that are followed with members of the administrative staff, have effectively diminished the capacity of the policy and administrative leadership **and** the profession to perform required functions. For example, limitations that prevent building principals from convening teachers to carry out the collaborative work required for effective schools have no place in collective bargaining contracts, but they are occasionally there nonetheless. Similarly, contractual agreements with building principals can have the effect when school buildings are closed of creating "surplus principals" who must be slotted to the first available building-level vacancies whether or not their specific skills or proclivities match the needs of the new setting. This can prove to be a serious impediment to effectively administered schools.

§ The "Benefits" Arising from Past Gender Discrimination No Longer Avail the Profession - Virtually all occupational and professional categories are finally available or are opening up to women. The extent to which education benefited because of prior gender discrimination is now suddenly removed, and the profession must compete for personnel in terms of its real status instead of a "protected" one brought about by discrimination formerly present in other occupational categories.

§ Teaching is Not a Profession - Despite the levels of education required for entry, teaching is not a profession in the true sense of the term. It lacks consciousness of its own particular knowledge base, it is insufficiently collaborative in its processes, and it lacks the power and authority to control essential dimensions of its functions.

§ For Teachers, Incentives for Career Advancement Lie Outside of Teaching Itself - As a career, teaching is strange. Advance cannot occur within the teaching role. In fact, the only way progress can be made (outside of that which is made through seniority) is by training for and assuming specialist or administrative (i.e. nonteaching) roles.

§ Education Is a Fragmented Societal Function - Responsibility for education is diffuse and fragmented and there are few powerful unifying influences. Policy authority rests in local and State boards and State and national legislatures. Teachers are trained in institutions of higher education. The so-called organized profession, that is, teachers, powerful because of its sheer size, is itself divided organizationally.

§ Education Is a Very Heavily Regulated Societal Function - The extensive regulation of education is itself evidence of the deep public concern for its quality and purposes. That regulation is undertaken by local boards, collective bargaining agreements, State boards, State administrative authority (through elementary and secondary school standards, teacher certification rules,and funding formulae, for example), the Congress, the Federal executive departments, and the courts. The extent and diversity of regulatory sources make fundamental improvement a very substantial task.[6]

§ The Root Causes Are Themselves Entangled - Careful examination of the root causes identified above will reveal one more key factor; each contributes to the strength of the others. Low status and low income are intimately connected as both are to defensive strategies by the organized profession. Regulation is a response to fragmentation, education's low status is in part associated with its being identified as a female occupation, and so on.

This brief analysis should make it clear that the Nation's educational problems will not yield to isolated or uncoordinated policy initiatives. Neither will progress be achieved if we persist in acting on the basis of perceptions of the current situation (including how we in education view ourselves as professionals) that obscure important realities, thereby rendering them inaccessible and untreatable.

The policy debate so far has focused on popular but quite limited solutions. Three that seem to have sparked the most public and political interest are merit pay, master teachers, and increasing the fundamental salary base of teachers. Other proposals like a longer day or school year have also drawn interest but on a smaller scale. These proposals have dwelt essentially on just two elements of the puzzle -- incentives for qualified persons to enter and stay in teaching and the attention of pupils on the prime tasks of schooling. Other "solutions," for example, those essentially proposing to turn over the education of children to untrained amateurs,[7] well intentioned as they may be, have all the earmarks of deepening the problems of schooling under the guise of improvement. Proportionately little of the discussion has dealt with issues of reallocation of the present resources, either as to what teachers do or how they are organized to do it. Few of the proposals deal with the basic assumptions underlying the system or the root causes of its current troubles. This one will.

THE PLAN OF THE ESSAY

The essay contains four distinct parts. Chapter One presents the concept of the organizing principle of inquiry. Chapter Two discusses impediments which seem to stand in the way of the proposal. Chapter Three offers glimpses of projected consequences for the educational system if it moved in the directions proposed.

Part Two of the essay, in effect, circles back to explore in greater detail the elements of the proposal. Chapter Four offers examples of inquiry processes and products for education. Chapter Five explores the several purposes of inquiry for education. Chapter Six discusses characteristics of behavioral and social inquiry in support of educational practice attention to which must be paid in the training of teachers and other educators and in the organization of instruction. Chapter Seven describes views of the ways in which the more formal inquiry processes of the research and development sector for education can improve the effectiveness of educational practice.

Part Three of the essay offers concrete suggestions on how the transformation could be brought about. It is presented in the form of fifteen memoranda to key roleplayers in the education arena ranging from Governors and Chief State School Officers to teachers, heads of teacher education, and education writers in the popular press. The memoranda present specific action steps as well as further views of the implications of the proposed reform for the roleplayers addressed.

Part Four summarizes the proposed reform, anticipates possible counter arguments, and sketches out the long-range promise.

Part One

INQUIRY AS THE ORGANIZING PRINCIPLE FOR EDUCATIONAL
REFORM IN AMERICA: PROPOSAL, IMPEDIMENTS, AND PROSPECTS

CHAPTER ONE   INQUIRY AS THE ORGANIZING PRINCIPLE FOR
                 EDUCATIONAL REFORM IN AMERICA

The root causes of the dissatisfaction with schooling in America will not be neutralized or removed easily. They present complex interlocking, mutually reinforcing constraints. What can be done?

Every once in a while a dilemma emerges whose solution lies in re-examining and re-ordering basic assumptions. This is one of those times. The assumptions requiring examination and change are those which have guided the societal support structure and the evolution of education.

The basic operating assumptions on which instruction in the Nation's schools, colleges, and universities has in the past been grounded are not difficult to identify. They have been:

1. Reliance more on the intrinsic satisfaction of working with young people than on fair financial return or high professional competence;

2. Seeing teaching as essentially the transmission of content;

3. Reliance on academic training, extremely modest internship, and, mainly, extensive individual experience as the preparation approach for teaching in both lower and higher education.

These three assumptions, in effect, mean that America has treated teaching as if it were a performing art rather than a true profession.

It should be apparent, both from the review of the root causes and the public clamor over dissatisfaction with schools, that the assumptions articulated above will no longer carry education where it needs to go. The times have changed; schooling needs to change with them. Instructional assumptions and technologies suited to the 19th century will not serve the needs of the 21st! Unless we change our basic assumptions the two century mismatch will continue.

This essay proposes to change not the purposes of American schooling but the assumptions which underlie its professional technique. That new set would include the following:

1. In preparing professionals and in undertaking instruction, educators ought always to act on knowledge about teaching and learning.

2. Systematic and reflective inquiry ought to become the underlying

professional frame of mind that guides teachers, administrators, teacher educators, and policy officials in the daily conduct of their responsibilities.

3. The products of inquiry required for more effective service are practical and immediate as well as theoretical and conceptual. They include the rationales connecting recommended courses of action to intended outcomes as well as the invention of techniques, materials, and prescriptions designed to achieve those outcomes.[1]

The organizing principle for educational reform in America must be unyielding commitment to the proposition that the profession of education seeking effectively to serve its clients[2] will train for and act consistently and continuously on what can be warranted as known.[3] Unless educators adopt this course, real and lasting improvement will elude us. Instead, limited by the current assumptions guiding the organization of schooling and the low-power instructional approaches that organization fosters and supports, the crisis created by the discrepancy between our educational aspirations and the insufficient outcomes of schooling will only deepen.

The assumption that instruction ought to be conducted on the basis of what can be warranted as known means that the Nation's teaching professionals, in higher education and lower, must assure that, in their day-to-day teaching responsibilities and in the training and retraining of professional personnel for those purposes, they everywhere conduct themselves according to the processes and products of inquiry very broadly defined. Broadly defined means that inquiry is not an activity going on just in academic and other specialized research settings but is a frame of mind embracing a comprehensive set of functions and responsibilities characterizing and informing the minute-by-minute, day-to-day existence of practitioners in education as well. Inquiry includes any form of systematic questioning or creative behavior that follows specifiable rules and that leads to verifiable, warrantable, or otherwise justifiable insights, actions, or outcomes.

The terms "warranted" and "known" are of crucial importance here. Warranted refers to the ideas of justification, evidence, and the importance of the quality of rationale or argument. It implies judgment, not merely technical skill. The term known refers to the concept of inquiry, the generic name for a diverse set of processes aimed at establishing what can be said to be verifiable or valid.

What would this proposal mean? What are its implications for practice and for the preparation of teachers and other educational professionals? At a conceptual level considerable attention would have to be paid to what it means to know and inquire as a practitioner. At a practical level educators must address what it is that needs to be known by practitioners, and how practitioners acquire that knowledge in their initial preparation and in the course of their careers in professional practice.

WHAT IT MEANS TO KNOW

The knowledge required for effective, warranted practice is of several different kinds. Some of it is conceptual, typically the product of formal inquiry in academic and related settings. Some of it is quite practical, derived from the specifics of given instructional settings and circumstances. Some of it is neither conceptual nor practical but contextual. Referenced here is the kind of knowledge which practitioners must have of those whom, in partnership, they serve. Such knowledge pertains to differential goals and contexts that lend essential meaning to the experiences of those in formal learning settings. The differences between these three different forms of knowing and the special characteristics of processes aimed at knowing in any of the three senses described here are explored further in later chapters.

WHAT DO PRACTITIONERS NEED TO KNOW?

Defining the essential knowledge of educational practice would take far more space and time than would be reasonable for an essay such as this. Furthermore, it is a task no single individual could or ought to undertake; there are too many roles to encompass and the range of knowledge is too great. Still, the broad outlines can be sketched, especially for the prime role of teachers.

Teachers need to be liberally educated in the sense that they are freed from their own parochial viewpoints, and comfortable in their knowledge of the broader historical, social, and technological context in which they work as professionals and which constitutes the backdrop for the educational goals they serve. Teachers make dozens of choices daily in behalf of the educational aims of their clients. Such choices constitute a demanding responsibility requiring breadth of preparation, sensitivity of view, considerable creativity, great perspective, and good judgment.

Teachers also need to have an absolute command of their subject matter. Content mastery is part of the knowledge required.

The responsibilities of teachers require all to know the intellectual underpinnings of their profession. Teachers must be familiar with human growth and development, normal and abnormal patterns and characteristics of human learning, and the social functions of schools. They need to be familiar with the organizations of schooling and the development of their profession. They need to be able to understand the philosophical roots of their craft, especially those bearing on the crucial value issues associated with schooling[4] and its goals. They need to know the political structures for education and have some appreciation for the manner in which society financially supports its educating functions and institutions.

The intellectual underpinnings of education serve as the lead-in to the last important body of knowledge teachers require, the professional and pedagogical knowledge of their craft. Teachers need to be deeply familiar with such content as the principles of curricular design, the techniques of instruction and its evaluation, the management of student behavior, the organization of schooling, and teaching's legal and professional obligations. Furthermore, teachers need to be skilled at conducting practical forms of inquiry aimed at illuminating the specific characteristics and requirements of learning and teaching in the constantly shifting circumstances of their daily work.

Knowledge bearing on the practical inquiry skills of teachers is crucial. These are the skills that equip teachers to understand who they are teaching, with what degree of fidelity to intent, and to what effect. These, too, are the skills which contribute directly to their creative responsibilities, especially of curricular and instructional design, whereby teachers match resources and actions to the learning needs of those in their charge. In an inquiry-grounded educational system all practitioners, teachers or principals, would require knowledge and skills to assess their own current performance, the specific needs of children, how to fulfill those needs and why, how to tell whether what was done was that which was intended to be done, how to know when to stop what one has been doing, and how to recognize and behave responsibly, ethically, and productively when, in fact, in a position of **not** knowing. Those are inquiry strategies of the most fundamental practical importance.

HOW DO PRACTITIONERS ACQUIRE THEIR KNOWLEDGE?

The answer has three facets. One has been suggested above in the emphasis on inquiry skills associated with practice. The second pertains to the initial professional preparation. By implication, that preparation ought to be keyed to the several requirements of the different kinds of learning and knowledge -- background, conceptual, content, contextual, and practical.

The third facet has to do with assumptions about the development of professional and conceptual knowledge not directly associated with initial preparation or the requirements of immediate practice. Research and development leads to new understandings and new capacities. Absent explicit attention to continuing professional development respecting research-based innovation, teachers can only hope to function at the level of their initial preparation as refined by their own immediate experience. No profession can afford to be satisfied with such an approach to professional development. All true professions provide in one fashion or another for this third facet and so, too, must education.

IMPLICATIONS

Reorganizing education on the principle that knowledge and inquiry are foundational has profound implications.

1. It provides the basis for establishing sets of criteria against which training programs and professional performance can be evaluated.

2. It will require a substantial increase in the resources for and revision in the structure of teacher preparation programs.

3. It forces a thorough-going reconceptualization of schools as places where professional service can be rendered.

4. It demands substantially increased investments in research and especially development in support of education.

5. It requires and provides incentives for recruitment of more capable people to teaching.

6. It provides a framework within which the performance of schools and the profession can be assessed and continuous improvement assured.

The remainder of this essay explores the meaning, effects, and implications of the proposed change in basic assumptions. Though it may perhaps sound unexceptional to propose that educational practice be grounded on what we know and what we can learn, our current operating assumptions are quite different. Those assumptions have led to salary structures, training approaches, and organizations for schooling that are largely antithetical to the kind of effective performance in schooling that the public and our times require.

The current system virtually precludes the approach called for here. Teacher training programs are woefully undersuppported[5] and only in recent years conceptualized sufficiently to serve the complex requirements of teacher preparation. Incentives, both financial and intellectual, are insufficient to recruit the calibre of personnel desired. Overwhelmed by the structural constraints of schools as currently organized and operated and irresistible pressures at the State and local level to deliver services without appreciable investment in their continuous evaluation and improvement, practitioners fall back on the tried and true, the old nostrums, or the patterns observed or applied to them when they were pupils themselves.

Perhaps the major implication, therefore, of a proposal to adopt the organizing principle of inquiry in schooling is the need to restructure schools so that they become places where professional teachers with organizational and peer support can strive ever more fruitfully to carry out their instructional and related responsibilities.

The ongoing assessment of instructional capacity and performance against the ceaselessly shifting requirements of instructional circumstance is not something that can be accomplished in today's atmosphere of professional isolation. Schools must be restructured as places of professional employment to provide sustained support for increasing understanding of the specifics of instructional need and possibility. They must become places where the resources of instructional staff can be pooled and assignments shifted as needs and opportunities arise. They must become organizations continuously receptive to developments and advances occurring elsewhere.

Systematically changing the basic assumptions underlying our professional craft will take a generation at least. Some of the individuals and organizations currently in place will be able to transform themselves, but the greater part will continue to function as they have in the past. But new practitioners could staff new schools: gradually, responsibly, more effective, inquiry-grounded models will take hold.

Fundamentally transforming an entire profession happens infrequently. The opportunity presented arises from the juxtaposition of public concern, societal need, and the improvement of basic understandings about human learning and effective teaching. It is an opportunity that can be seized now. Still, there will be major impediments to overcome before these assumptions can be installed and their benefits realized.

CHAPTER TWO   **PROBLEMS IN SUPPORTING EDUCATION ON THE PROCESSES AND PRODUCTS OF INQUIRY**

A proposal to embark on a lengthy and closely articulated professional reconceptualization based on inquiry must examine related experience. Why, if the reform is so desirable and valuable, has it not happened before this time? What needs to be overcome if the projected benefits are to be realized? In the last twenty years directed efforts to improve education through research, development, and related activities have met with less than overwhelming success. Why, and what impediments to reform need to be addressed and removed?

The answers to these questions are not neat and clean nor are they always comfortable to confront. The explanations double back on one another, seemingly defying neat categorization. Still, some initial ordering seems possible.

THE RESEARCH/PRACTICE GAP

One of the most tired cliches in the literature of educational innovation is the so-called "gap" between research and practice. The gap exists, all right, but it is much more than just between research and practice.

One aspect of the "gap" is education's own uncertainty about its knowledge base. The concept of esoteric knowledge (that is, knowledge understood by the specially initiated or a very restricted group) is central to any profession. The key notion here is **knowledge,** not merely language or jargon.

Education's uncertainty about its own "esoterica" may be shown in a few anecdotes. A leading researcher in the field of teaching and teacher education, N.L. Gage, recently wrote a book, The Scientific Basis of the Art of Teaching,[1] that by rights should have been in the hands of virtually every teacher educator and every teacher trainee since its publication. Published in 1978, the potential audience, therefore, was in excess of 800,000 teacher trainees and teacher educators. At an October, 1982, meeting of the Association of Colleges and Schools of Education in State Universities and Land Grant Colleges Gage revealed that fewer than 5000 copies of the book had been sold! The message is loud but not necessarily clear; either teachers don't feel the need to learn about the scientific basis because they already know, they believe it is unimportant, they don't care what it is, or they are not aware of their need to know.

Consider other examples. In the September, 1982, issue of Phi Delta Kappan the superintendent of a major American urban school district makes the blunt claim that there is no esoteric knowledge foundation for pedagogy.[2]

Finally, consider an event at a meeting of teacher educators in a major industrial state. A keynote speaker addressing the knowledge base for teacher education was asked for clarification of the concept. What is it, he was asked. Give examples. When the speaker responded, in part by listing the names of the major presumably well-known researchers and synthesizers whose work encapsulated significant portions of the knowledge base, he was interrupted and asked to recite the names more slowly so they could be written down! The level of awareness of the intellectual underpinnings of the craft cannot, under such circumstances, be said to be very deep.

A second and third aspect of the research/practice gap have to do with the inadequacy of the results of formal inquiry and its insufficient scope. Criticism of the adequacy of knowledge (for example, consider the recent unwarranted assertions made by leading researchers based on a study purporting to compare the relative performance of private and public secondary schools)[3] leads to unwillingness to use the results of formal inquiry because of serious doubts respecting the validity of the conclusions and recommendations drawn from the work.[4] The insufficiency of the knowledge base, on the other hand, refers to the fact that given the dimensions of the problems educators face, the amount of research undertaken to date is simply less than the tasks require.

A fourth part of the explanation for the existence of the gap is the differentiation of function which now characterizes education with respect to inquiry. Inquiry is carried out now mainly in universities, specialized research institutions, and the policy agencies in and bearing on the education establishment. To that extent there is a gap simply by virtue of where the work is done and who does it. By definition it is necessary to figure out how to get results utilized because the results are in one place and the potential for utilization is somewhere else.

What is a fact, however, has assumed the status of a prescription. Teachers and administrators do not see themselves as researchers or even as inquirers. Those functions are seen as being reserved for the academics of highest order (i.e. "the graduate faculty") whose sophistication and training in complex and sensitive methodologies makes them the only ones suited to the work(!). Such beliefs, of course, become a self-fulfilling prophecy whose implications go well beyond the performance of research. Practitioners come to believe (and, in truth, they are not discouraged in so doing by their professional peers of high academic rank in the university setting) that not only can they not **do** research but they cannot understand, critique, or otherwise gain access to its mysteries. And again, the practitioners are not far from being wrong here, not only because they lack training, capacity or perhaps both, but because the modes of reporting research and related work that academics have chosen (or are encouraged) to follow virtually assure distancing from practitioners. The "cognitive maps" in the minds of the several elements of the education profession get in the way of better connections between the research community and practitioners; this is not a wholly accidental phenomenon. In a low status profession like education (see below) one of the ways it is possible to acquire status, at least in one's own eyes, is by asserting and maintaining status differentials. A certain amount of that happens in education.

The consequences of the differentiation go even deeper. Graduate faculty in most institutions where research is carried out typically do not work on the initial preparation of teachers. They work with graduate students; in education, as Harry Judge has observed, most graduate students are engaged in advanced preparation programs whose purpose is to prepare people for non-teaching roles in education.[5] Thus, the faculty who are most knowledgeable about current academic and scholarly research and methodology bearing on education are removed from teacher training. The gap caused by differentiation of function and, to a lesser degree, the concern for status, actually causes the removal of those most knowledgeable; what might otherwise assure the conceptual awareness of each successive new crop of teachers to the research state of the art is thus not available to them.

The gap also exists because of under-recognition of the different epistemological foundations of academics, practitioners and the clients of schools (cf. Chapter Six). The problem is not exclusively one of academics not "speaking" to practitioners, policy makers, or the public. It is also that practitioners and others who daily confront the complex realities of life as it is lived experience surprise, incredulity, and impatience, even, at the results of formal inquiry. They dismiss its relevance without recognizing or appreciating its contributions. During my government experience, especially with legislative and political figures, I was quite surprised at the extent of the skepticism with which social scientists were greeted (a skepticism often briskly reciprocated, I might add). Candidly, my first reaction, too, was not very tolerant. It was not until some years later that I came to appreciate the significance of the divergent perspectives scholars and legislator/politicians bring to their work on the same puzzles which nevertheless lead them both to try and relate to one another. The contrasts owe not so much to variant purposes or intents as to the distinct ways in which each knows what they know. It is not that either is wrong or right but that they are different, each tending to be confirmed by the demonstrable success experienced in his or her own domain.

Practitioners, too, have ways of asserting the primacy of their own epistemological foundations, the power of what they know and the ways they know it. What our European colleagues now refer to as scientific imperialism finds reverse expression, no less hegemonic in its character, in the oft-heard practitioner riposte to the academic: "You ought to get out here and spend a week with us to see what it's **really** like!"

There is another source of the research/practice gap. At least part must be attributed to a certain lack of capacity. The data respecting who, on the average, has been attracted to the profession, both in teaching and teacher education, are in. The results are not flattering to educators as a group. Surely at least **part** of the research/practice gap must be explained by lack of capacity to appreciate the subtleties, sophistication, methodologies, and concepts associated with the practice and processes of formal inquiry. What might happen to upgrade present capacity given opportunities to learn, however, is quite another matter.

Finally, part of the research/practice gap now perceived to exist between different sectors of the larger educational establishment may be a **knowledge/practice** gap resident in **practitioners.** Referenced here is another version of the old saw about the farmer who, urged to learn more about improved farming techniques, retorted he **already** knew how to farm twice as well as he was!

Part of the non-application of concepts known to be important can be explained by characteristics of schools (see below) and the nature of the tasks teachers are called upon to perform. But part is also an outcome of knowing more conceptually than we have figured out how to implement from a practical perspective. Consider the examples offered in succeeding chapters about differential learning rates, sensory modalities, and learning styles. The problem arises not because of the inaccuracy of these concepts but only when a teacher or administrator seeks to act differently on them. Is the time available? Will the organization of the class and school permit it? Are the instructional techniques available? Are materials sequenced and designed to match the modalities and styles of the learners? Do the schools have the materials? Are they easily accessible to the teachers? The answers, in the main, are no, nor is there any immediate prospect that anytime soon it will be possible to answer such questions in the affirmative. Teachers cannot be faulted for this shortcoming. It is a case of knowledge outstripping practice because of the failure to invest sufficiently in the equivalent of engineering for instructional practice, to consider the structural impediments to more effective, knowledge-based practice, and to assure adequate supplies of support materials.

THE ORGANIZATION OF SCHOOLS

The isolation of practitioners from one another is another serious bar to more effective service and professional status through inquiry. The "business end" of education -- teachers and principals -- undertake their day-to-day responsibilities only rarely, if ever, having a chance to work with or observe one another. Isolated from one another physically, in self-contained classrooms or in buildings removed from one another, teachers and administrators have next to no opportunity to seek or render mutual counsel, an essential, practical form of inquiry. In contrast, the detailed records of the medical profession, to say nothing of the common practice of consultation and secondary review of diagnoses and treatments (even if only by other non-physician parts of the medical establishment, e.g. nurses, medical technologists, or physicians' assistants), provide opportunities for professional dialogue only marginally available to teachers and administrators. The legal profession has equally effective, though different, forms of interaction and continuous review. This capacity is found in the records of the court system, legal consultations, and the adversarial character of much legal practice and appeals procedures, all of which assure both interaction and review of professional performance.

In fact, neither schools in America nor the education profession as a whole are organized on the assumption that there is an existing or developing knowledge base for instruction and education nor are they organized to support the kinds of inquiry practitioners ought to be engaging in daily better to carry out their responsibilities and achieve their appointed ends. What does it mean to say these things? Again, illustrations help.

If American schools were organized on the assumption that, over time, new understandings and techniques worth attending to would emerge of which teachers and administrators were obliged to learn, then continuing professional development would be seen as a primary obligation of the working day and the schools would be organized accordingly. But they are not. Districts provide so-called inservice days, typically, one to three a year; few of these, however, are geared to new knowledge or otherwise acquiring facility with the products of inquiry. The school day certainly does not provide an opportunity for teachers or administrators at the building level to engage in ongoing professional development as part and parcel of their daily responsibilities. On the contrary, classroom teaching and meeting the day-to-day obligations of running a school do not include such expectations. In the "profession" of education such activities represent gifts of out-of-school-time by inadequately paid people who often have to support associated cash costs out of their own pockets! Unlike the bulk of the argument which is directed to all segments of the education profession from schooling through the higher education components to the more narrowly construed research agencies, the present comments are oriented primarily to observable shortcomings of the structure and organization of elementary and secondary schools. Research organizations and, in the main, institutions of higher education do, in fact, define professional responsibilities as including ongoing expectations of continuous professional development, and provision is made for same in the work environment.

Indeed, most of the people reading this volume will not be teachers. Ask yourselves how your continuing professional development is provided. Most of the readers are expected to make provision for their own development as part of their daily responsibilities and have sufficient authority and autonomy to do so; furthermore, large portions of its fulfillment, in fact, comes from direct daily interaction with people you consider your peers. None of these options is available to teachers or principals. That bears thinking on.

It should be apparent after a little thought that the "flat" organizational structure of schooling with its virtual total isolation of teaching and building-level administrative staff from one another would have another serious shortcoming. It would effectively deny practice-oriented inquiry from being exposed to the multiple perspectives (see the more extensive discussion of this in Chapters Four and Six) so important to sound social inquiry (even if there were time and expectations to engage in it). Diverse epistemological foundations and the importance of access to multiple perspectives mandates the conduct of behavioral and social inquiry, especially of the decision-oriented kind, in a collaborative manner. That does not mean that all work must be done in teams; individual efforts would still be possible, but before or during the conduct of inquiry considerable consultation ought to take place. If the professionals in schools do not see one another in the performance of their responsibilities it is highly unlikely, practically speaking, that such consultation, either with colleagues, clients, or the representatives of clients, will take place. In the absence of such collaboration, inquiry is likely to be flawed.

THE LOW STATUS OF EDUCATION

More than a few of the impediments to realizing the benefits of inquiry for profession has to be affected by its reward structure, and its reward structure is clearly related to its status. Low status has other consequences, too.

For example, low status can find expression in the form of diminished attention, expectations, and resources to do the job. On the last, for instance, how else are we to explain why teacher education throughout America has struggled with inadequate support to accomplish the clinical training function for which it has been responsible? How else are we to understand the continuation of the practice of awarding temporary certificates for untrained persons to enter teaching even though in recent years there has been a surplus of certificated graduates? Why haven't colleges and universities as the parent organizations of teacher education programs confronted more directly the problem of qualifications of teacher training candidates? Why don't colleges and universities exhibit the same expectations concerning inquiry and scholarship for teacher education that they do for the arts and sciences or other professional schools under their purview? Why, when one would assume that college and university presidents would be quick to recognize their crucial role in support and service to lower education in the Nation, has that responsibility so frequently been ignored and sometimes been expressed in active opposition to efforts to upgrade the teacher education enterprise? These questions are asked rhetorically, recognizing they may not be directly answerable, but they do suggest areas and priorities requiring attention, especially from the broad perspective offered by the proposition advanced here.

Reasons for the low status of education as a profession abound. Inadequate salary incentives, perceptions of the lower qualifications of present and entering personnel, the devaluation of children and those who care for and work with them, and judgments that educators don't do anything, really, that any parent doesn't do daily are partially to blame. The absence of mystery about the workings of the profession (because the overwhelming majority of the adult citizenry has twelve or more years of experience in "the system" and thus feels qualified to make judgments about it), widespread views that in recent years the organized profession has pursued its own self-interests with greater zeal and steadfastness than it has its obligations to its clients, and lingering consequences of its being perceived as "women's work" (and thus subject to the persisting problems of gender bias in our society) are also major constraints operating on the profession of education which contribute to its status problems. Still, current circumstances cannot be allowed to diminish either attention or effort toward more desirable states of affairs.

The status accorded the profession of education, however, has been more than shared by that of the domain of educational research and development itself. There are many reasons.

One of these must surely be the relative maturity of the enterprise. As an activity deemed worthy of national support, for example, educational research and development is only a little less than thirty years old. But youthfulness as an organized pursuit becomes an unsatisfying explanation when the history of the growth and the developing purposes of the support over those thirty years are examined closely. Gradually increasing Federal dollars, for example, from the mid-fifties until a substantial increase in the mid-sixties, was then followed by a leveling off. The seventies, however, marked a sharp decline in support which continues to this very day. (The already reduced appropriation levels for the National Institute of Education are now slated for further reductions in the coming budget year.)

Why has this happened? How do status considerations figure in this checkered history? Are there other factors as well (besides the obvious economic difficulties the Nation has been facing and the attendant requirement that tough priority decisions be made and accepted)?

Certainly part of the explanation lies in some of the matters already referenced, for example, misplaced expectations of what formal inquiry can accomplish because of inadequate understandings about its character. Conversely, on the miniscule scale on which it has been advanced, what **could** research achieve? How quickly can a system of schooling organized as it is respond to what is learned through inquiry? The belief that inquiry is for academic and similarly situated people and not for the practicing profession is still another element. But major responsibility must be lodged in the scale of effort in the research and development sector. That is the outcome of priority judgments that have to correlate closely with status assessments.

Consider the comparison of the medical and education establishments in America, enterprises of roughly equal size. **Research in medicine is supported nationally at a rate 72 times that of education!** In such a ratio we see profound manifestations of a status and political priority judgment. We are insistent that physicians act on what is known and that they learn ever more to fix the things that go wrong with us. Former Commissioner of Education Frank Keppel once explained the relative investments in medical and educational research thusly: no one, he said, ever died of a split infinitive. Like many metaphors, however, it begins to crumble when one thinks of the little deaths that occur daily in schooling as achievements that might have been made are not. Consider the consequences of progressive non-achievement for citizenship, employment, family life, the economy, and the national well-being, to say nothing of a sense of personal fulfillment or the deepened appreciation for the meaning of life.

The extremely low level of support for educational research and development nationally, given the reasonable expectations generated at the time of its expansion in the mid-sixties, especially the important steps taken to reinforce and expand the institutional framework for the conduct of educational R&D, has contributed to pre-existing squabbles that have occasionally arisen within and between the educational research community, the National Institute of Education, teacher education, and the organized profession. Jerald Zacharias, the M.I.T. physicist and educational developer/innovator, once remarked that academic fights were so vicious because the rewards were so small! A parallel explanation might well be offered to explain difficulties that have plagued educational research, particularly its Federal management and the crucial appropriations process. If the research, practitioner, and research management communities cannot present a unified front on what they are about, why, and how, small wonder that the enterprise finds difficult sledding in this time of great financial stricture. The basic problems are small size of the inquiry enterprise caused by the low status it shares with its parent profession coupled with insufficient awareness of the characteristics and requirements of educational inquiry (again, see Chapter Six). These are matters over which educators themselves can have a great deal of influence if they inform themselves and choose to act.

NOSTALGIA, COMPLACENCY, AND FEAR

Discussion of the impediments to productive impact from the processes and products of inquiry broadly defined is not yet exhausted. Nostalgia, complacency, and fear must also be acknowledged.

Nostalgia works in several ways. Parents and others addressing schools often seem to present a posture which seems to say that "what was good enough for us **then** is good enough for our children **now**," or "I want the institution of schooling to be something I can **understand**, and what I **understand** is what I **experienced**." Comprehensible from a human point of view, this stance represents a real challenge to the profession. Elements of that client posture respecting schools have great legitimacy; the guardians of children must be able to understand at some level the schools their children attend and, more, must feel comfortable with them. But insofar as the posture denies the real changes that have taken place in the functions of schools, in the knowledge underpinning professional practice, and in the society for which it is being performed, then nostalgia constitutes a substantial but not unconquerable impediment to grounded improvement.

Complacency on the part of the profession is also perfectly understandable. None of us, even those engaged in the functions of change and improvement, is accepting or enthusiastic about changes if they mean alterations in the ways of working which have become comfortable to us. Furthermore, when a profession like ours is under stress, both as a result of the ceaseless criticisms (no small portion of which is as arrogant as it is ignorant) and the profession's own intrinsic nature, then resignation or complacency may be, perhaps, better understood, even if not justified.

Fear is quite another matter, however. In the face of the implications of the processes and products of inquiry, fear may be legitimate or unwarranted. It is legitimate when one's role is threatened. It is unwarranted -- though perhaps no less real in its individual effects -- when the changes it points to can, in fact, be accommodated through appropriate responses.

Teachers may be afraid that they may not have the capacity to perform according to the guidelines suggested by the outcomes and processes of inquiry, perhaps because of limitations of ability, training, or both. Institutions may feel that the implications of proposals like this one will have the effect of taking them out of contention for the performance of functions for which they have traditionally been responsible and which have contributed to their livelihood. (Part of the proposal several years ago made by the Salishan Deans, for example, spoke to the likelihood that teacher education institutions with insufficient critical mass of faculty fully to reflect the scholarly underpinnings of teaching would ultimately have to relinquish their training responsibilities. This brought howls of protest, some of which quite rightly pointed out that larger-staffed teacher training programs were not reflecting the knowledge base any more conscientiously. The only credible response, of course, where such is the case, is that the larger programs should be required to fulfill the expectations of knowledge adequacy or also close up shop; size itself is meaningless!) Finally, fear may be wholly warranted and lead to responsible avoidance behavior, like fear of the dangers of thunderstorms on North Carolina's Neuse River which justifies rapid and effective evasive behavior when signs of one approaching first appear. An implication for change which is unlikely to be feasible because of uncontrollable circumstances or unrelievable constraints may most properly be avoided lest unrealistic expectations arise that only contribute further to the already unenviable position of the profession.

The first step toward coping with fear, of course, is recognizing it for what it is and distinguishing between legitimate fears, unwarranted ones, and plain old healthy anxiety.

WHAT IF EDUCATION WON'T YIELD TO INQUIRY?

I have left for last one important remaining "impediment" to realizing the benefits of inquiry. That is the possibility that educational practice will not yield to inquiry.

Suppose the complexity is too difficult or fluid to unravel. Suppose it is impossible to encompass all the relevant variables. Suppose that the capabilities of the professionals in the system will not permit either engaging in practical inquiry or capitalizing on the results of inquiry done elsewhere. Suppose the difficulties caused by the characteristics of behavioral and social inquiry discussed in Chapter Six -- e.g., value embeddedness, ubiquitous metaphors, and contrasting epistemologies -- prove to have been the reason why inquiry has been so difficult to conduct and apply in education. Then where does the proposition advanced here go?

With tongue only slightly in cheek I would note only that the last line of the preceding paragraph full of potentially devastating suppositions, is itself a question to which inquiry strategies can be applied. Those who would reject the overall argument advanced here should still be required to defend their alternative proposals by demonstrating how they are grounded on knowledge and justified by sound argument. In the long-range interests of steadily advancing improvement, what other approach could conceivably be justified?

* * *

Some readers may perceive the messages in this chapter as "hard." Of course they **are** because they deal with impediments and shortcomings. The chapter, therefore, would inevitably seem critical. It may be seen as implying that one or another agency or actor that ought to have been accomplishing "x" was not. Professionals who would like to believe they were engaging in sound practice from the perspective of the organizing principle offered here may have been operating in seriously flawed ways.

The usefulness of the analysis offered here, however, can be tested by two criteria: Is it justified by the evidence and the logic? Does it cover the territory (i.e., is it even-handed in addressing the impediments wherever they may be found to lie)? On both counts the answer seems to be yes.

CHAPTER THREE   **PROJECTED OUTCOMES AND CONSEQUENCES**

Notwithstanding the circumstances that have so far impeded efforts to improve the effectiveness of schools and colleges through the processes and products of inquiry, the existence of this volume clearly signals the belief that the impediments can be overcome and that real benefits at acceptable cost, dollar and otherwise, can be achieved. What are those benefits, consequences, and costs?

MORE EFFECTIVE SCHOOLING

More effective schooling has to be the most important objective of the proposal advanced here. The logic is compelling.

1) If teachers and administrators know more about the nature of the objectives they are trying to achieve in the complex, diverse social and cultural contexts in which they are teaching,

2) if they know more about the nature of human learning and how to stimulate it and have a firmer and more conscious grasp of the content and cognitive skills for which they are responsible,

3) if they have more effective materials and techniques generated by their own initiative and that of others,

4) if they are more continuously aware of when they are effective and when they have not yet been so with individual children,

5) if they have the time and the other resources to be reflective and evaluative about their performance, and

6) if they work in settings which encourage and support collaborative efforts,

then children they serve will learn more that will be of value to them and the larger society.

The logic alone is compelling, but there is a second reason why this proposal should increase student achievement. Educators have been aware for some time that the "hidden curriculum," that is, the basic structure of the school, its mode of operation, and its organizational features, has a powerful effect on the outcomes of schooling for individual children and groups. Organizing on the principle of inquiry will turn schools into **learning institutions**; the inherent character of the entire enterprise will precisely parallel the objectives of the professionals for the children and youth in their charge.[1]

BETTER RELATION TO DIVERSE STAKEHOLDERS

Education has one characteristic as a profession that makes it quite different from the highest status professions of medicine, law, or engineering. That difference lies in an important observation, namely, that educators do not have clients (although I have used the term in this essay because I have not yet found a better one) in the same sense as the aforementioned professions.

The word client has two meanings. One indicates a status of dependence. The second means customer. Neither, as David Seeley points out, adequately describes the desirable relationship of educators to those they serve.[2] For one thing, children and adults will learn (but what?) whether they come to educational institutions or not. Second, teachers and administrators do not themselves accomplish the objective of effective service. On the contrary, it is the learner who does that. Successful achievement of our aims is measured ultimately not by what we do but by what those **whom we serve** can do after we have finished working with them. Successful service for educators, therefore, entails working in **partnership** with those who come to us, engaging in "common effort toward common goals."

Full appreciation of the character and benefits of behavioral and social inquiry should contribute directly to the enhancement of the necessary partnerships in education in service of a pluralistic society such as ours. Much though some critics of American schooling might wish otherwise, individuals and groups bring varying images and attitudes about the purposes of schooling. Most are not absolutist about the different desires they possess; virtually all are ready to accept partnership in a society defined in terms of our longstanding ideals as a Nation. But the differences are crucial to the commitment and the meaning of schooling for the children who come. To the extent that awareness of the characteristics of behavioral and social inquiry sensitizes educators to values, metaphors and multiple perspectives, then the proposals advanced here should enable us to work far more effectively with education's many stakeholders -- individual, community, cultural, societal, and corporate.

JOB DIFFERENTIATION WITHIN TEACHING

One of the certain concomitant outcomes of grounding the profession of education on the processes and products of inquiry will be the development of hierarchically differentiated structures for teaching.[3] The outcomes are said to be concomitant because differentiation will follow from the increased sophistication of professional understanding, but it is also a necessary pre-requisite for the performance of inquiry by practitioners.

As conceptual and professional understanding deepens, the diverse inquiry functions required in individual school settings will become more apparent. Those functions will relate to curriculum design, instructional planning and evaluation, parent relations, minute-by-minute decisions respecting instructional strategy, as well as the provision of the various expertise required in academic and other instructional content. Existing expectations that each teacher be skilled at all aspects of the complex responsibility of "keeping school" will certainly give way to some form of specialization.

Differentiation of function, of course, does not necessarily require a hierarchical structure. The likelihood of a hierarchical arrangement arising owes to two considerations. The first is the need to organize and allocate tasks. Once differentiation occurs, someone who is deeply familiar with the basic tasks needs to be called upon to see they are organized and coordinated. Second, if the promise of continuing professional development as part and parcel of the working day is to be realized, then one of the differentiated functions (and a higher order one at that) has to be performing the important linkage function between the school and the advancing professional and conceptual world "out there" supporting education. If the "lead teacher" has that linking function, then the continuous re-development of currency in awareness and performance can be accomplished integrally with instructional planning and evaluation.

The emergence of a hierarchical ordering of roles will also have the important additional impact of creating the career ladder **within** teaching that will permit the most capable and committed to advance, and to be paid commensurate with their broader and greater responsibilities while continuing to lend their skills to teaching **per se.** Task differentiation should also constitute an important recruitment incentive to teaching as well.

INCREASED CAPABILITY OF EDUCATORS

Here the focus is on qualifications and capabilities **per se,** not on other relevant matters like career paths and financial incentives. The proposal advanced here should contribute to the improved capabilities of the professional staff in two ways. The first is by the growth that will occur as teachers and administrators learn through practice-based inquiry how better to serve the students in their charge. Inquiry processes applied daily in schools will constitute the most important ongoing staff development instrument possible.

Second, as college students consider their future career, especially the collaborative way in which they might be working in schools redesigned to facilitate the inquiry demanded of practitioners, they will find teaching a profession of gratifying service, yes, but, as important, one taking place **in an environment of intellectual stimulation.** That restructured professional reality should attract the intellectually able; it will keep them once they get there.

On both counts, an inquiry-based profession should lead to increased practitioner capability and quality.

TEACHER EDUCATION WILL BECOME A POST-BACCALAUREATE ACTIVITY

Grounding the profession on the processes and products of inquiry will mean, among many things, careful attention to the knowledge foundations of the teaching act. It will become even more apparent than it is now the four-fold requirements of a liberal education, content mastery, the intellectual underpinnings of the profession, and the practical (including inquiry) skills of the teacher cannot be completed in a four year program. Almost certainly a 4+2 sequence will be required for entry into teaching and an additional two years of formal study in such areas as curriculum design, instructional evaluation, staff development and supervision, practical inquiry processes and so on required for those with aspirations to become lead teachers.[4]

It is enough for the baccalaureate program to carry responsibility for imparting a thoroughgoing liberal education and to assure mastery of the content area to be taught. By liberal education, incidentally, more than just a mere distribution of offerings is meant. Teachers require more than simply knowing a little about a lot. The responsibilities of teachers in a technologically advanced free society require a firm knowledge of the present circumstances of their own society and culture and its aspirations and how it relates to others in the world. They require the capacity to communicate effectively with adults and children. Teachers must know how the human community develops and applies knowledge. They must have inquiry skills and be capable in the complex set of skills we refer to (perhaps too easily) as problem solving and decision making. They must be able to function in the world of values, have a developing sense of their own world view, and, most importantly, have become conscious about the need for, and the most comfortable approaches to, their own continuing learning in the future. That comprehensive set of objectives plus mastering content area seems more than enough for the baccalaureate program. Demonstrated success in these respects ought to be the criterion for **admission** to an intellectually rigorous and clinically grounded professional preparation program for teaching of at least two years if the requisite conceptual, technical, and practical elements of the role are to be thoroughly imparted.[5]

Program and admissions will change, but so will the settings where it takes place. Full appreciation for the complexities of the training responsibility will lead to the creation of highly sophisticated clinical sites for training teachers. Under the true joint control of the higher education institution and the cooperating district, teacher training clinical schools will permit the detailed observation and provide the clinical support functions necessary to accomplish the training aims.

UNIFICATION OF THE NOW DISPARATE ELEMENTS OF THE PROFESSION

In the past considerable valuable energy has been deflected from the improvement of service and the advance of the profession by occasional struggles between important sub-sectors of the profession. The organized profession, teacher education, local districts, the broader higher education community, and State authorities have far too often found themselves at odds with one another. These disagreements owe a great deal to the different perspectives of the role players respecting their several responsibilities but also to perceptions of their relative importance that may not be wholly warranted by the facts.

When the characteristics of inquiry broadly defined are more widely appreciated and inquiry's role more widely shared within the profession, the effect on the whole should prove unifying. What has previously been seen far too often as a set of distinct (though articulated) responsibilities will come to be seen as differentiated functions supporting a common theme. That theme will come to be seen as an orientation which fundamentally organizes and reflects the professional role. More than that, however, its unique importance in the maintenance and enhancement of a free society as **the model, functionally and institutionally, for what individual citizens in a free society need to be able to contribute to sustain and enhance the whole social and national fabric** is likely to emerge with greater clarity.

GREATLY IMPROVED RESOURCES FOR FORMAL INQUIRY IN EDUCATION

As the understanding and application of inquiry processes and products spreads throughout the profession, claims for additional resources in support of the subsector of formal inquiry (research and development) in the profession will increase, and those claims will come to be answered. There are several reasons.

The first is that a unified profession will actively support appropriation requests. Second, if the work undertaken reflects self-consciousness about the characteristics of behavioral and social inquiry, then the way it is done and presented to legislators will lead to a more sympathetic hearing. Third, the responsiveness to ultimate stakeholders (that is, the non-professional partners of schooling) likely to emerge from widespread attention to the knowledge underpinning the practice of teaching will lend additional political energy to requests to support such activities.

ADDITIONAL COSTS

The "bottom line" is always relevant. What would the proposal advanced here cost?

Additional investments, relative to current costs, would be marginal, not radical. The main additional costs would be those associated with the adequate support of the professional training programs, with the marginal investment of paying the higher salaries of the lead teachers in the differentiated staffing model, and, finally, with the cost of the additional investment in formal research and development.

Calculating the additional investments that will need to be applied to the professional training responsibility for education should not prove difficult. Other clinical training programs at the post-baccalaureate program will provide cost models. There will be some additional costs, to be sure, in establishing the jointly controlled (university and school district) sites for clinical training to provide the settings and the kind of clinical supervisory support for student and beginning teachers that the new knowledge-based, inquiry-rich training models will require. Full implementation would probably entail no more than a 25 to 40 percent increase in the current investment in teacher education which now ranks, however, at or near absolute bottom of per capita student costs at the baccalaureate level!

The second cost factor associated with this proposal has to do with the additional salary of the lead teachers. (I assume that raising the base salary paid teachers needs to be addressed in **any** proposal for reform and, therefore, feel justified in excluding its costs in calculating the marginal costs of the proposal advanced here.) Assuming that the differentiated staffing model results in requiring one teacher in eight to be trained and advanced to the role of lead teacher at a salary of $8-12 thousand more per year in recognition of the broader and heavier responsibilities, the net additional cost to the current investment in teachers' salaries would be something on the order of eight percent (based on a presumed average salary of $20,000 per teacher times eight teachers as the denominator and the full $12,000 as the numerator). Actually, a case can be made that offsetting amounts to that percentage will come from the diminished professional responsibility of the building administrators on the differentiated staffing model envisioned and the greatly reduced need for consultants and supervisors in central administration since the roles they theoretically now perform would be almost wholly subsumed by the lead teachers' responsibilities.

The remaining source of additional cost would be the support required for the research and development sector for education. A reasonable projection would be its expansion over the next two or three decades until it reached a level of support for all its many functions approaching two percent of the annual national investment in our educational systems.

Can the outcomes described in this chapter be achieved? Yes, but before considering how this might be done it will be helpful, first, to circle back and explore in greater detail examples of inquiry for education, its purposes and characteristics, and views of how, especially, the more formal kinds of inquiry, namely research and development, can come to improve educational practice.

Part Two

THE USES, PURPOSES, AND CHARACTERISTICS
OF INQUIRY FOR EDUCATION

CHAPTER FOUR   THE USES OF INQUIRY FOR EDUCATION

Education can improve its effectiveness -- and become a true profession -- by systematically striving to rest what it does and why on the processes and products of inquiry. The proposition stands or falls, ultimately, on the prospective uses to which inquiry can be put and the results of that application. This chapter seeks to illustrate the uses of inquiry in support of education. These illustrations show how many academic disciplines contribute to the understanding of education, schooling, and instructional practice. They show how inquiry is directed at knowing **and** doing. They suggest how systematic inquiry can be the stimulus for productive change. They point to the basic differences in what it means to know and imply, therefore, variety in the purposes, methods, and frames of reference in terms of which inquiry proceeds. The examples have been presented as a basis for making two central points. First, the range of activities included under the label "inquiry for education" should be viewed very broadly. Second, the examples provide an opportunity in the next chapter to examine somewhat more analytically the purposes of inquiry for education.

EXAMPLES

Consider the examples offered below:

§ Presenting curriculum content through the classic medium of the printed text inadequately reflects either the diversity of learning styles present in individual classrooms or the variety of pedagogical approaches required to convey the concepts and skills intended. A curriculum project is commissioned to develop a multi-media, comprehensive, validated set of sequenced materials for classroom use the effectiveness of which in every-day instructional settings can be attested to through documented evaluation studies.

§ Seeking to determine the worth and justification for continued or expanded appropriations for categorical programs at the Federal level, officials undertake formal evaluations of the outcomes of such programs as the old Title I or Head Start. Assuming the programs will continue at some level in any case, they design the studies not only to support judgments about continued support but also to improve the program in the future.

§ An equipment manufacturer, convinced of the worth of computer based instruction for young children, commissions studies aimed at better designing keyboards and display equipment for simplicity and durability in the hard-use environment of a school classroom.

§ Status studies of the performance of children of different cultures, socio-economic status, or abilities in heterogeneous or homogeneous groupings offer guidance for the future assignment of children to a classroom or school.

§ Seeking to test or refine cognitive learning theory, an educational psychologist designs and carries out studies on short and longterm memory.

§ A school district needs to replace the materials it has been using to support beginning reading instruction. It surveys its primary teachers, principals, and supervisors for their views of specifications for the replacement materials, forms a representative committee of knowledgeable practitioners including those responsible for staff development in the district, and undertakes a careful examination of the available materials.

§ Three members of a school district citizen's advisory group conduct a key-term search of the Educational Resource Information Center (ERIC) data files on the topic of local school site budgeting. On the basis of perusal of the abstracts, they read more than seventy documents and conduct telephone follow-up in search of newer and more fugitive materials. On completion of the review of all materials, they prepare a summary of their findings for the use of school officials, teachers, and laypersons involved in the district's local site budgeting initiative.

§ An elementary classroom teacher, learning disabilities specialist, school psychologist, principal, and parent convene to review the results of the multi-factored assessment of a learning disabled child and to prepare an appropriate Individualized Educational Plan (IEP).

§ Test developers write prospective questions for mathematics proficiency examinations. They evaluate the validity of the questions by inserting them in current examinations. The returns are analyzed, revisions made, and re-evaluations conducted. The test items are ultimately cleared for use in future examinations.

§ School officials collect survey results from students, teachers, principals and parents. They seek perceptions on school achievements and needs. The surveys are periodically subjected to analysis on a district-wide and school-by-school basis for insight into present climate, evidence of the achievement of district or school goals, or clues to the emergence of concerns possibly requiring attention.

§ A team of sociologists conducts observational studies of children at play in and out of school settings. The objective is to further understanding of the values and norms exhibited by children from diverse cultural settings and the extent to which those norms are affected by the school environment. What is learned from such studies may prove helpful in understanding the nature of possible conflicts between school-connected norms and values and those norms and values children bring with them to school. Findings may be instrumental in defining teacher education curricula and more effective instructional and classroom management strategies.

§ An anthropologist "shadows" a school principal for several months. The objective is to examine in microscopic detail the demands and influences impinging upon the principal, the tasks requiring completion, and the dynamics of the role and its occupant. The study could contribute to recruitment and career choices, provide a template against which principal training programs might come to be defined, and afford a point of comparison with other administrative roles in and out of education. It could perhaps lead to deliberate attempts to modify the principal role in the interests of improved efficiency and effectiveness.

§ Economists and school finance experts, working from computerized information descriptive of the current status of a State's educational system, explore the consequences of alternative models for subsidizing public education. As variables like pupil/teacher ratio, numbers and proportions of children with special needs, indicators of metropolitan service burdens, local property tax rates, administrator/teacher ratios, and the like are manipulated, the differential effects on school districts throughout the State can be calculated as a basis for determining finance formulae.

§ A student, previously functioning well in school, begins to display less desirable characteristics in both achievement and approach to school learning tasks. Direct observation and work with the student does not yield clues productive of constructive strategies. After preparing a thorough work-up of the basis for undertaking further examination of the matter, the teacher schedules a parent conference to explore possible non-school variables that may explain what is happening to develop approaches, possibly in partnership with extra-school resources including the parents, that might be employed.

§ An historian undertakes an examination of the diaries of frontier women to enrich understanding of the role they played in family dynamics, socialization processes, and the educational development of children in non-school settings. Together with work on the leadership role played by women in more formal educational settings which had been previously ignored by historians, a revised picture of the past alters our conceptualization of our present, that is, the school-climate, instructional practice, family, educational policy, career advancement, and societal variables currently at work.

§ A study of the passage of an important piece of education legislation illustrates the dynamics of key actors, timing, effective and ineffective strategies, and the interplay of interest groups. Future policy makers in and out of education can compare past experience with plans formulated for emergent legislative needs.

§ A team of educators, anthropologists, and child psychiatrists explores in great detail the relationship between non-instructional variables, student achievement, as well as non-school outcomes. The study contributes to the understanding of the importance of school climate variables emerging from (or not directly related to) purely pedagogical concerns and how such variables might be more productively employed in the school setting to enhance student achievement. The findings have bearing on individual school settings as well as on pre-service and inservice professional staff preparation programs.

§ Faculty members construct a teacher education program on the basis of their understanding that children from different cultural groups present diverse cultural norms and values in the pedagogical setting. Didactic materials together with clinical and field-based experiences are arranged as instructional means in service to the necessary intellectual, skill, and attitudinal goals. The approach is tested and revised until teaching candidates achieve the desired outcomes.

§ Significant differences may exist in the form and nature of moral development as between so-called "masculine" and "feminine" styles (not to be equated with gender-specific developmental outcomes). This knowledge in turn leads to explorations of the extent to which the values and norms embodied in classroom and school management strategies may subtly enhance or interfere with the learning and development of children in the school setting.

§ Examination of the character of the academic disciplines that form the starting point for much of the formal, academic research undertaken in support of learning, schooling, and education suggests that its analytical orientation yields knowledge tending to support the achievement of certain kinds of educational goals as contrasted to others. If the underpinning knowledge supporting school practice comes from patterns of inquiry more compatible with analysis, where does the knowledge contributing to the development of skills and goals associated with capacities for synthesis come from? Such work suggests the importance, for example, of educational research arising from the arts and humanities, expressing and providing understandings that complement the more analytical contributions of the behavioral and social sciences.

§ Teacher education faculty and administrators, teachers, school administrators, State officials, and laypersons are separately convened in parallel to develop new standards for approving teacher education programs in a State. Each group works from a common outline, but their independent efforts (including the rationale for the proposals advanced) are shared week by week with all the working groups to keep everyone fully informed of the developing ideas. The final products from all the working groups constitute the raw material for the development of a comprehensive set of standards for teacher education in a State.

§ Increased research and development activities in education together with a greater commitment on the part of leading teacher educators to reflect the knowledge base in pre-service training programs culminate in the development of extended programs for teacher education through expansion of the curricular and clinical components of the existing models of teacher preparation programs.

§ Studies of attempts to stimulate productive change in school settings reveal the importance of active involvement of practitioners in the identification of the need for change, the validation of the proposed innovation, and the development of the strategy for undertaking it. Such studies have important implications for research and development policy, for the organization and administration of improvement efforts on the local scene, for research and development training programs, and for the examination of the epistemological underpinnings of educational innovation and reform efforts.

§ Teaching teachers about language development in hearing impaired children has always been difficult because of the inability to display sequences taking place over extended periods of time. The possibilities of marrying computer technology to the video disk open up new opportunities. Videotapes of language behavior collected over time can be edited, sequenced, and computer coded on the video disk. Using programmed instructional techniques and inquiry processes, students can view and predict language development sequences, receiving immediate feedback on the accuracy of their predictions. The unique combination of immediate feedback and instantaneous access permits dramatically increased efficiency of instruction, reducing instructional time from two full quarters to less than a month. The prospective applications for laboratory instruction without laboratories and for instruction in the visual and musical arts, as a minimum, are overwhelming.

TWO PERSPECTIVES ON THE USE OF INQUIRY PROCESSES AND PRODUCTS

This chapter began with illustrations of ways in which inquiry processes and products could ground educational practice. Before turning to an analysis of the purposes of educational inquiry and consideration of its characteristics consider two more views on how inquiry can relate to practice.

Examples of Inquiry Processes/Products Pointing in Several Directions

We know that children learn at different rates, according to different sensory modalities, and that different people have or develop "styles" of learning that seem to work for them. The implications of such understandings extend in many directions.

The instructional strategies of teachers, the organization and character of curricular materials, the placement of students in classrooms, and the organization of those settings, to list just four, would all be affected by such understandings. Knowledge does not fit in one place only, like a puzzle piece. Its implications extend in many directions and may be susceptible to many interpretations and configurations.

Consider a more precise example. Research has documented (legitimized) what all parents and other observers of children and young adults know, namely, that peer influences are very powerful. The response to that knowledge, however, depends upon one's perspectives, attitudes, and purposes. Some, seeing such influences as negative or at best diverting, would seek to minimize them. Others would attempt to utilize their power in the learning setting. Some would focus on classroom management strategies; others would attempt to define learning tasks in ways which would incorporate the mechanisms of peer processes to challenge students and enhance their learning. The direction of the impact of knowledge is not foreordained.

Consider a third example. The mix of students in learning settings can influence outcomes. Research indicates that heterogeneous groupings of children on racial, socio-economic, and ability bases can have important beneficial impacts along several different dimensions of achievement -- cognitive, social, and attitudinal. Acting on the basis of such understandings, however, requires more than just determining how to get the proper mixes of students in given settings. Clear goals become important as guides to the professional staff. Teachers and administrators must understand the differences that exist among the learners and what those differences might conceivably mean in a learning setting. For example, differing norms likely to exist in diverse cultural and socio-economic groups must be attended to when settling upon the frames of reference within which instruction will take place and student behavior encountered. Advance consideration needs to be given to potential problems that might arise as children are re-grouped so that neither teachers nor administrators are caught unaware.

An Example of Many Points of View Affecting One Setting

A last example is multi-directional, not in the sense that a concept arising from scholarly inquiry leads outward in more than one way, but in the sense that the multiple perspectives arising from inquiry work back on singular settings for learning however they are put together.

For example, what goes on in the classroom must be viewed in light of what is known about human learning, a great portion of which is illuminated by research from educational psychology and learning theory. Classrooms are also social systems, however, and as such they can be fruitfully understood growing out of work in sociology and social psychology. Classrooms can be understood as power and authority structures, a perspective illuminated by the discipline of political science. Renewed interest in the classroom as a cultural system expressing roles, norms, and values of its own as well as encompassing those brought by the individual members has been explored helpfully by anthropologists.

The above represent a sampling of contributions from the **academic** sector. Other insights and techniques have come from more applied work in instructional practice, curricular design, behavior management, the study of the professions, law, and the organization and administration of education.

Teachers and administrators cannot afford to be unaware of **any** of these understandings unless, of course, we are content to accept an educational system staffed, essentially, with more or less talented amateurs distinguished from other college graduates on the street only by career choice, their own particular individual experience in schools and colleges, and the willingness to forego the economic return other persons with such educational attainments might expect to earn. What is actually required, of course, in the way of intellectual capacity and professional training to be able to handle the multiple perspectives forthcoming from behavioral and social inquiry in support of education and to be able to work in such complex professional settings is, in terms of the current organization and incentive structure of teaching, quite another matter.

CHAPTER FIVE   **THE PURPOSES OF EDUCATIONAL INQUIRY**

Some of the more frustrating and disappointing squabbles in the educational research and development domain have wrestled with the purposes of educational inquiry. What should be in and what out? Is a piece of work more appropriately called research or evaluation? Is a project "development," "demonstration", "school-based innovation," or "local site problem solving?"

The view advanced here, as the examples provided in the preceding chapter clearly illustrate, is a very broad one, indeed. Any form of questioning or creative behavior that follows specifiable rules and that leads to verifiable, warrantable or otherwise justifiable outcomes should be included. After all, this essay's purpose is to help formulate the fundamental reconceptualization of an entire profession. It is more universally to extend inquiry and the frame of mind it represents to the thinking and behavior of a group far broader than academics and other formal researchers. In that context, the purpose is inclusive rather than exclusionary.

DISCIPLINE-BASED/KNOWLEDGE-ORIENTED

A great deal of the inquiry and scholarship now undertaken in hopes of ultimately supporting instructional practice and education flows from the academic disciplines, especially the behavioral and social sciences, but in recent years from the arts and humanities as well. The purpose behind such inquiry is not action but understanding. While nothing has happened recently to falsify the old truth that there is nothing so practical as sound theory, the purpose of inquiry conducted from the disciplines is not doing so much as it is knowing.

From psychology we can approach the many processes of learning "inside" the individual human organism. We seek to understand how learning takes place, what its effects are, how it can be measured, what forms it takes and how those forms may differ from one another. Psychology also offers tools with which to explore interactions among individuals as participants in learning and educational settings. It contributes to the design of instructional materials and strategies and the organization of classrooms and schools. More recently, cognitive science, emerging principally from psychology but drawing also on neurology and researchers working on artificial intelligence, is furthering our understanding of thinking, learning, and mind, all centrally related to the furtherance of the aims of educators.

Sociology affords a different perspective. Sociology studies social organization and structures, hierarchies, and the operation of norms and values in society. It contributes to our understanding of the operation of class and family structures in schooling and education, to the analysis of formal and informal group behavior relating to education, and to the analysis of role definition, expectation, and performance in schools and other educational settings.

Anthropologists illuminate education by exploring it as a cultural phenomenon. In the macro sense they study the function of education and educational institutions in the larger culture. In the micro sense they look at classrooms or schools as cultures of their own, following patterns of behavior, norms, and relationships sustained by their members.

Economists study the relationship of education to economic goals. They help education understand its relative importance in the larger society as a consequence of the analysis of the investment of national wealth in the enterprise and, through the analysis of resource allocation, gain an appreciation of where and what we value, as institutions and as a society. Economists are also concerned with human resource development. In recent years, the contributions of economists to educational evaluation studies, especially on a very large scale, have been quite substantial.

Political scientists study power - who gets what, when, where, and how. Clearly, education, schooling, and even instruction can be viewed meaningfully in terms of power and its manifestations. From the particular perspective of political science we can learn about the formulation and implementation of policy decisions, as well as the organization and impact of interest groups, legislatively and administratively, on policy issues.

The arts and humanities, in contrast to the behavioral and social sciences, contribute more holistic perspectives in terms of which educational phenomena can be viewed. The behavioral and social disciplines in the main approach their objects of study analytically, dissecting phenomena into observable or manipulable variables, attempting to understand the relationships that exist among them. The arts and humanities present a somewhat different orientation, in many respects closer to the way laypersons view things, as wholes. This characteristic makes them especially useful because of the frames of reference they contribute for defining and understanding educational goals and objectives.

Historians contribute to our understanding of the present by illuminating the experience of the past. Their work contributes to the delineation of the context within which we operate enabling us to understand continuities and discontinuities, present and emergent.

Philosophy contributes to our ability to analyze arguments, concepts, values, and the epistemological (knowledge) foundations of the education enterprise. Philosophers help us come to terms with the basis for our ideas and the connective tissue between them.

In practice, of course, a great deal of formal educational inquiry is interdisciplinary. The academics who conceptualize such work and carry it out understand that the phenomena they are studying do not conform neatly to the boundaries of one or another discipline. They know that the very fact of labeling the work they do as "educational" research implies an ultimate intent of leading to some practical benefit, even if that benefit may not be immediately specifiable or even remotely likely to be of immediate utility.

Some years ago a publication sponsored by the National Academy of Education formulated a framework for distinguishing various kinds of education inquiry from one another.[1] It suggested that a useful distinction would be to speak of conclusion-oriented and decision-oriented inquiry. That terminology is still helpful, especially in the present context. Discipline-based work as described here is almost always conclusion-oriented, aimed at increasing understanding of phenomena with little intent of contributing directly to decisions or practical professional behavior. This is not to suggest, however, that it is of little consequence to practitioners. On the contrary, it is essential to background understanding and full appreciation of the context in which practitioners operate. To make the distinction between conclusion-oriented and decision-oriented work leads directly to the next major category.

DECISION-ORIENTED

Specify the kinds of decisions that can be made in support of education and you have specified the categories of decision-oriented inquiry. They are several. A first partition would be to distinguish policy decisions from practical or operational decisions.[2]

Policy Decisions

Mindful of the old saw that "whatever is done above you in the organization is policy and whatever is done below you is operations, and your job is to rationalize and productively connect the two" (i.e., policy and operations are highly relative to position and role), it still makes sense to distinguish between policy-level decisions and those decisions that properly constitute the exercise of professional practice. Respecting policy it seems further to make sense to distinguish two broad categories of concern, the first pertaining to matters currently being addressed by practice, the second to concerns that might prospectively be addressed.

A great deal of the inquiry done in support of existing policy is properly called evaluation research.[3] One fruitful distinction drawn regarding evaluation research is that between **summative** evaluation, or that which is undertaken in order to determine the worth of something (and, by implication, whether it should be continued, expanded, or reduced), and **formative** evaluation, that which is undertaken in order to come to judgments as to how and what to alter in order to make a program, approach, or practice more nearly fulfill desired aims. Summative and formative evaluation are undertaken in respect to programs and policies either under way for some time or, at least, begun.

Prospective policy calls for inquiry which may look at existing programs and practices (e.g., studies which illustrate either non-achievement of desired goals or unwanted outcomes as a consequence of existing arrangements) or it may entail examination of circumstances external to the educational enterprise to demonstrate the need or desirability of formulating new goals and programs or new approaches to achieving them.

Whether oriented to existing or prospective policy, the frame of reference for decision-oriented inquiry is defined, not as in discipline-based or
conclusion-oriented inquiry by the perspectives and interests of the inquirers,
but by the perceived needs of the decision makers and the influences working
on the decision makers causing them to attend to the policy concern in the
first place.

The inquiry that takes place may or may not conform to the rules of the
academy. That does not make it any less a form of inquiry. For example, a
legislative inquiry into program management follows certain rules of evidence and
procedural logic that have a form and rigor all their own. It may or may not
proceed through the systematic collection and analysis of data in a researcher's
sense. For example, the rules may deal with timeliness, constituency as well as
stakeholder access, opportunity for thoroughness of exposition and the like. Because
such rules can be defined, of course, doesn't mean they are necessarily followed any
more than sloppiness or error is avoided in academe.

Policy inquiry, of whatever kind, seeks to establish indicators of need as
against performance. It seeks to establish and verify connections between present
practice and either desirable or undesirable outcome. In the rich panoply of present
circumstance it tries to identify pathways that offer superior promise. It may seek
to define goals and objectives that will enlist commitment, mobilize constituencies,
or secure the allocation or reallocation of requisite resources.

Practical Decisions

The inquiry most ignored by those in educational research is the inquiry
that takes place in practice. That it should be ignored is a bit of a mystery.
My own view is that the inquiry of practice has been ignored, under-recog-
nized, or denied in some measure because of needs in a low status profession
to establish hegemonies which allow those doing the establishing to assert or
feel higher status and, therefore, greater comfort. If the reconceptualization
of the profession proposed here is ever to be implemented, this is a reality
which needs to be confronted head on. Academics have tended to look down
upon practitioners in education as less capable, less sophisticated, and less
knowledgeable. Though it may never have been intended, it seems apparent
that one of the ways higher education has gone about preserving that sense of
superiority has been to lay claim to the tools and strategies of inquiry and
deny the performance of parallel or analogous activities by practitioners.

Nevertheless, in education there are two broad categories of practical
decisions. The first category focuses on the kind of inquiry called for in
actual instructional situations. The second category embraces all the inquiry
needing to be done to support instructional acts and those responsible for
undertaking them.

Inquiry in Instruction. Teachers potentially engage in inquiry dozens of times
daily. Much of it is diagnostic in character. Monitoring classroom climate -- the
feel of the instructional situation -- is a form of such inquiry. Continual assessment of the progress of individual students or groups of students is another.

Assaying what is going on in a particular situation where desired outcomes or processes are not occurring as intended is still another. Materials are chosen through inquiry processes. Instructional approaches are selected, changed, modified, all on the basis of inquiry strategies of one kind or another. I do not mean to imply that because practice **might** proceed according to a process of inquiry more or less formal (even if applied on a less than conscious basis) that all teachers or even a majority of teachers **now do so**; if the profession were so to define itself, it might **come** to, and, therefore, begin to train and expect performance accordingly.

Recognizing such professional behavior as inquiry is something of a radical act. Such behavior is usually seen as planning or problem solving but rarely inquiry. Identifying it as inquiry is deliberate, a step taken not only because it is a fair description of the generic process that ought to be followed, but because doing so establishes what could be a powerful unifying principle for all of the now diffuse, discrete, and disparate elements of the education profession.

To think of successful teaching as requiring practice-based and practice-directed inquiry is not intended to obscure real differences in the orientation of that inquiry or its purpose. Teachers are at bottom concerned not merely to **know** but to be able to **do**. This basic orientation to practice places a premium on the instrumental value of knowledge, especially as it is useful for the creative processes of design guiding the actual delivery of instruction.

Conceiving of teaching in this way is consistent with views emerging from the careful analysis of the teaching act, especially the work done in recent years at Michigan State University and by people trained there. For decades the profession, in its practice and in its training arm, has acted in the belief that teaching was essentially a rule **applying** behavior. Under that view what teachers do is test situations (itself a form of inquiry, I would point out, however) to determine which rules to apply and then apply them. Under the emergent conceptualization, the profusion of variables in any instructional circumstance, the complexity of their relationships to one another, and the evanescent character of their configuration make teaching far more rule **generating** behavior than rule applying. Good rule generators must be good inquirers.

Inquiry Supporting Instruction. Just as instructional acts are the product of continuous processes of inquiry, so are the instructional act and environment supported by inquiry of many different kinds. As the examples in Chapter Four suggested, inquiry may have to do with evaluation of instruction, needs assessment of many different kinds, and the inquiry processes associated with resource selection, acquisition, and installation. Materials selection, professional staff development, and other forms of professional planning are all processes that ought to be undertaken in an inquiry frame of mind.

These inquiry processes take place at the department or building level (e.g. curriculum design), at the district or college level (e.g. materials selection or evaluation of learning outcomes), or beyond (e.g. definition of program standards for teacher preparation programs or elementary and secondary schools, or the state-wide analysis of staff development obligations, for example, created by legislative initiatives as in the passage of the Education of All Handicapped Children Act).

Conceiving of such practice-related activities as inquiry even though they may also be seen as planning or program development activities, invites attention to the data or knowledge on which the activities are based and the quality of the argument or rationale which justifies the course of action ultimately settled upon. Careful grounding of such actions on the basis of verifiable data, valid knowledge, and justifiable arguments assures a secure foundation for professional action.

Development

A third inquiry activity embraced under the larger decision-oriented category is development. Development is akin to engineering. The objective of development is, on the basis of theoretical principles and understandings already established, to design, construct, and then test materials, techniques, organizational structures, equipment, and the like intended to carry out or achieve instructional or educational functions or objectives.[4]

What distinguishes development as an inquiry function is the way it is conducted. The theoretical knowledge guiding the project is consciously held. The objectives are carefully specified. The qualifications of the participants in development reflect both the underpinning knowledge and the characteristics of the professional user population. The procedures for formative evaluation on the basis of which successive revisions are to be undertaken are explicitly defined.

More specifically, the objectives of development defined in this way include such resources as instructional techniques, curriculum, instructional equipment, instructional organizations, evaluation instruments, and diagnostic tests. A specific example, drawn in this case from the curriculum area might be helpful. Suppose that an area of current scholarly knowledge, deemed to be insufficiently represented in materials available for school use, for example, anthropology, is selected for attention. Suppose further that the proponents of this projected curricular area seek to develop materials which fully reflect two prime concepts emerging from a long line of research in cognitive psychology. Different children learn according to different sensory modalities; presenting materials through multiple sensory modalities should increase the strength and richness of the learning achieved. Second, the systematic inculcation of cognitive inquiry strategies in instructional practice not only serves to achieve higher-order cognitive process learning goals but makes the learning more interesting and effective for the pupils.

The development team in such a case would be composed of anthropologists, cognitive psychologists, curriculum designers, teachers, media experts, and experts in instructional evaluation. Curricular goals would be established. The outlines of the curriculum would be sketched and the first materials designed and constructed. Initial trials would be subjected to intensive evaluation by the developers, the students participating as subjects, and perhaps other observers. Of special concern would be the extent to which the materials achieved the pre-defined instructional objectives. Initial evaluation would be followed by revision and re-trial until the entire set of materials and their accompanying instructional processes achieved the goals intended. The project would not be completed until materials were ready in final form and until materials and techniques for carrying out any necessary inservice training of prospective user teachers were prepared (and validated as well). By past standards of investment in curriculum writing or teacher-made materials, the cost of development conceived in this way is very substantial, running into the millions of dollars. Amortized over millions of children, however, the costs are minimal.

The process described above, with appropriate modifications given the objective of the project, constitutes the generic development or engineering approach. Given the breadth of the conception of inquiry being advanced in this essay, however, sense can be made of the inclusion of still another activity as part of development, defined **just** as broadly.

The more familiar engineering concept of development was pioneered in domains founded on the natural sciences. We speak easily of development of electronic, communications, or weapons systems. We apprehend, at least at some fundamental level, the concept of developing a new vaccine. All of these examples and more that might be offered entail careful engineering toward specified objectives working with phenomena that are essentially external to (although they may be intimately connected with) the human behavioral and social organism. They rest on the physical, chemical, and bio-medical sciences. Insofar as one can define organizations, discrete instructional techniques, materials, physical environments and equipment, however, development or engineering can be meaningfully undertaken in the field of education as well.

I will advance the argument, however, that in education (and for that matter in other human service fields as well) what would otherwise be called continuing professional education or staff development ought equally to be considered a part of the **development** task, that is, part of decision-oriented inquiry. The argument is based on a generalization of the purpose of development or engineering processes as found in other fields. The more familiar definition of development is the systematic process of the creation of new products, materials, techniques, and processes, based on the theoretical and empirical understandings derived from science, which accomplish, according to pre-specified criteria, stated objectives deemed desirable. Generalizing from such a statement it would be possible to say that development is the process of creating capabilities to perform specified functions or achieve specified outcomes where that capability did not exist before.

The generalization is suggested by important differences in the production and delivery of capabilities derived from the natural and physical sciences and those derived from behavioral and social inquiry. Once a capability is demonstrated in electronics, materials engineering, or overcoming a specified disease, the further diffusion of the capability is typically distribution of a hard product.

For education, diffusion of innovation proceeds only partially through product distribution. Much more frequently, diffusing a new capability occurs through painstakingly **re**developing it in each of the members of a vast army of professionals who currently occupy teaching and administrative roles in our schools. Each teacher for whom the the new (skill) capability becomes a necessary professional tool must undertake a learning process (although not necessarily as extensive or as costly) and develop the capability in him or herself. The development process in education is not completed until the requisite skills and human capabilities have been successfully incorporated in the professional repertoires of practitioners.

How useful is this renaming of what we typically label training, staff development, or even dissemination? The objective is certainly not to create a new jargon. The re-definition is offered as a way of making a point, namely, that in considering the role of inquiry processes and products in support of education we cannot afford to make easy assumptions that the language and concepts of science -- so-called "big science" as undertaken in other domains -- will translate easily or neatly into the domain of education. The phenomena are different, the characteristics of the domain are different, and the definitions of science, inquiry, and the "technologies" derived from them will vary accordingly.

CHAPTER SIX   CHARACTERISTICS OF INQUIRY FOR EDUCATION

The preceding chapter concluded with a note of caution about carrying over too easily to education the frames of reference of science and technology applied to other sectors of society. The purpose of this chapter is to examine how the characteristics of behavioral and social inquiry -- academic or practical -- applied to education manifest themselves, why they do, and what the implications of those characteristics might be.[1]

The lack of deep familiarity with behavioral and social inquiry of this essay's primary audiences constitutes a real challenge. What is written must also pass the scrutiny of the research and development community which is (or ought to be) intimately familiar with the matters being addressed. In a sense the challenge of this chapter epitomizes that which faces all of social science seeking to support educational practice -- can its outcomes be translated in terms useful for practitioners and policy-makers?   Let the exposition begin with a story.

A STORY

Heather Fairbanks, a social psychologist by training, was also more than familiar with the other social and behavioral disciplines. Much to her surprise, she had been sufficiently stimulated by the remarks of President Elwood at the quarterly meeting of the all-university faculty to find herself still thinking about them in relation to a comment of her next door neighbor. The night before he had said that some of his students thought so little of themselves that it was difficult to engage them in the learning tasks of his seventh grade classes. President Elwood had talked about the university's obligations to the schools; Heather's own sense of obligation ran parallel but largely unacted upon.

She knew something of the literature on self-concept, its relationship to achievement, and its interactive nature with environment. Clearly, all three elements were suggested in her conversation with her neighbor Don. He was concerned about the outcomes of his students' achievement. He and his students were in the social context of a school. His own identification of the source of the problem was the low self-concept of the students.

The more Heather thought about it, though, the more she began to see a problem. What was she to look at? The character and quality of the instruction? Perhaps it was at fault leading to low achievement and thereby depressing self-concept. (She hoped not because she liked Don!) Maybe it was something about the environment in which the children found themselves outside of school. She knew some of the children Don was talking about because they lived on the block, but they had never struck her in neighborhood interaction as having poor opinions of themselves; indeed, to her they seemed quite full of themselves! And what about that elusive diagnosis, "a low self-concept?" What did that **mean**, anyway? Was it something that the children "had" or was it something ascribed to them? Did that make a difference? If so, what? Clearly, she would have to make choices about what angle she would take.

Heather quickly realized she had other choices as well. Presuming she could settle on a conceptual framework for looking at what was going on (e.g. psychological, environmental, or instrumental), she would also need to settle on a method of exploration. She could, for example, review the literature bearing on the chosen framework and try to develop experimental strategies that Don might employ as interventions to increase achievement **and** self-concept. A query passed through her mind: Is it the school's job to enhance self-concept? Would school authorities give her their permission for such an experiment?

She thought about the possibility of an ethnographic study in school, or in school and out. The time requirements of either approach would be substantial, the second doubly so. She thought about the possibilities of devising a questionnaire approach working with just the students individually, or in relation to one another, the instructional staff, their non-school environment, or some combination of several or all. What about the possibility of in-depth interviews with students and instructional staff to understand better what each meant by or revealed relative to "self-concept" to get a better grip on what realities students and teachers were encountering? As she ruminated about these things, the reminder triggered by her passing thought about permission from the authorities set her thinking about how the ethical responsibility of researchers to protect their subjects from harm or from having their privacy invaded might affect her design or the manner in which she approached her subjects.

On her way home she stopped in her office, picked up a couple of journals and the draft of her self-evaluation for the reappointment portfolio due next week, and started home. The new billboard for a local super-premium beer blatantly appealing to consumer status-hunger got her to thinking about audiences. "Who would I be doing this study for? To help Don? Maybe. To make a contribution to knowledge? Yes. To get me promoted? (Too late for the **reappointment** folio, unless I can get the design completed and inserted as evidence of current work, she thought to herself quickly.) Where can it be published? (Maybe I should think about that before I design it.) Maybe I could interest the school system enough to support it. That might require me to modify the design, though, in ways that will prevent me from finding out what I'm interested in or doing the work in a fashion that will earn the plaudits of my academic peers."

She pulled up in front of the house just as Don was coming off the front stoop for the evening paper. "Don," she said, "I've been thinking about what you said last night about your students. I've been trying to understand better what's going on but I've realized there are dozens of choices to make and I thought you might be able to help me think it through better...."

PRIMARY CHARACTERISTICS OF BEHAVIORAL AND SOCIAL INQUIRY

The Heather Fairbanks vignette serves to introduce discussion of the characteristics of behavioral and social inquiry. Many variables stand in complex relation to one another. Values issues abound. The purposes for undertaking the inquiry vary as do the frames of reference of the stakeholders.

Multiplicity of Variables

Inquiry processes and products in support of education, whether they are situated in the scholarly and academic community or relate to the policy and instructional domains of practice, must cope with a great multiplicity of variables. A variable is anything which might conceivably have some relationship to the object of study. For example, in a classroom the variables relating to the performance of the children in that class might include such things as the curriculum, the training and experience of the teacher, the physical arrangements, the mix of students in the class, climate variables in the school, contextual variables (like time of year, community factors, and even the weather), the organization and administration of the school, the family circumstances of individual children, whether or not they were adequately fed and clothed during the period of investigation, the social dynamics of the class and the like.

The listing is exhausting enough. Then consider that each of the "variables" listed above is itself capable of being further refined or broken down into composite elements. Curriculum includes goals and objectives, structure, sequence, learning processes, types of materials, instructional requirements, degree of flexibility, and so on. The social dynamics of the classroom include mode of expression of interaction, types of interactions, directional flows, out-of-class factors, gender/age/race dimensions, adult/child relations, whether or not employed or utilized as part of the learning situation or conceived as extraneous to it, and so on.

The story with which the chapter opened illustrates that same richness. The variables are seen to be in and out of school, maybe associated with the instructor and maybe with the students, perhaps keyed to psychological reality, perhaps sociological.

Whether research or evaluation is done for conclusion-oriented or decision-oriented purposes, the large number of potential variables is unavoidable. Academic researchers interested, for example, in the refinement of theory, may have the prerogative of finding ways to "control" variables through the manner in which the problem is defined or the research design structured, thereby carrying out the inquiry so that the effects of a given variable or variables are neutralized. The manner in which this is done, however, is of critical importance as is the argument or rationale justifying the chosen approach.

Those engaged in inquiry supportive of practice do not have the same luxury of attempts to control variables. The reality of practice, as an environment and as actions taken therein, simply does not often admit such a prerogative. If it does, it is to a far more limited degree.

Complexity

The multiplicity of variables involved in instruction and education together with the difficulty of control arise from and in turn constitute expression of the great complexity of the phenomena with which we are dealing here. The number of potential variables is but one aspect of the complexity though a vital one.

A second element of the complexity lies in developing images of the configuration of the variables. What relates to what and in what order or pattern? In part learning those configurations is the very objective of formal research; but it seems apparent that before unknown configurations can be charted, one must begin with what can already be established.

Matters are complicated still further, however, when one realizes that the configuration of variables that characterizes situation "a" may not function in quite the same fashion for situation "b." And if that were not enough, it can also be demonstrated that the interactions among variables may actually flow in more than one direction, that is, variable "a" may cause or enhance variable "b" which in turn works back on variable "a." Some concrete examples of these characteristics of social and behavioral inquiry may be helpful.

The complexity arising from the presence of so many variables seems fairly obvious. Consider, again, the number of variables in the example of inquiry on classroom learning. Developing a picture or schema of how the many elements operating on the learning task relate to one another is certainly not a simple task. When one considers, however, the manner and degree to which the specific character of the variables alters the dynamics that exist between them, then one can gain an appreciation of not only how difficult inquiry is in such settings but how complex a teacher's tasks are. A classroom made up of children whose stomachs are filled with nutritious food and who are clothed adequately for the season will exhibit quite different patterns of interactions among other variables than one in which all or some of the children cannot be so described. A school administered by a martinet filled with contempt or disdain for his teaching staff will have set in motion influences in (and out of!) the classroom which, once again, will alter the dynamic of many of the other variables.

To illustrate the way variables in instructional and educational settings can affect one another simultaneously (the term for which is an interaction effect), consider the example of Don's students and the relationship between student achievement and self-concept. Research has established that achievement and a good self-concept go together and, similarly, that low achievement and a low self-concept correlate. But what is the direction of the correlation? Does high achievement produce the good self-concept or does the good self-concept yield the achievement? The answer, of course, is both and it depends. (Of course, where one finds interactive sets of variables like the two just mentioned, these have to loom large for both researchers and practitioners because of the significance of working effectively with them or, conversely, avoiding a downward spiral of the two.)

Metaphorical Character

A third characteristic of behavioral and social inquiry is its metaphorical character. This is not an easy notion to communicate, but it is of crucial importance.

Metaphors are employed throughout science, but their use in behavioral and social inquiry is constantly encountered. Through the element of surprise or contrast, metaphors aid in both communication and the stimulation of thought; but they have an essential lack of fit, a certain murkiness that creates problems when pushed too hard.

Why does the metaphorical character of behavioral and social inquiry demand attention? What does attending to it mean? What are some examples?

Let me start with an example Herbert W. Simons used in discussing metaphors.[2] Take the word "substance." When we are asked what we mean by referring to the substance of something -- for example, the substance of an argument -- we usually mean its key elements, its core, or its essence (all, incidentally, metaphorical terms themselves. But consider that the word "substance" is derived from two Latin terms for standing under. In other words, the concept of substance acquires its meaning by referring to something outside or other, in much the same way that a boundary describes a territory without constituting the territory.

Take the word "curriculum" defining a course of study. In this sense course, meaning pathway or track, is also a metaphor (derived from the Latin root "to run"); but if one thought about not just the noun form of the track but the verb form "to run" or, better yet, "to course" (that is, to run swiftly), what images come to mind to stimulate understanding of what curriculum might really come to mean?

Almost any terms we use can be seen as having metaphorical dimensions -- reinforcement, reward, delinquency, discipline, classroom management, education, schooling, social dynamic, socioeconomic class, level (of education), school climate, knowledge base, research/practice gaps, and so on. The importance of understanding the metaphorical character of so much of our discourse about behavioral and social dimensions of instruction and education lies in what it tells us about how we can come to know things of importance for practice and, also, what it means to know. If, in fact, processes of inquiry in support of education do not yield "hard facts" or understandings of discrete substance and their relation to one another but, rather, diverse perspectives of greater or lesser utility, then realizing this ought to lead to somewhat more humility among and between researchers and practitioners and, maybe ultimately, greater collaboration as well.

Metaphors represent realities but do so only imperfectly; maybe even more importantly, as social science is increasingly suggesting, there are different realities corresponding to different metaphors and arrangements of same. Inquiry processes and products supporting education, therefore, cannot be conceived as precise keys fitting unchanging locks; they are more like successive approximations of multiple perspectives, each subscribing to differing but legitimate views of the reality being explored.

The implications of this conception of inquiry about instruction, schooling and education are profound. Researchers and practitioners undertaking and attending to behavioral and social inquiry in support of education will require sophistication of mind. They will need to display comfort in the face of ambiguity tempered by a commitment to educational and instructional goals. They will need to be receptive to equally valid alternative conceptions of reality. They must recognize that singular conceptions must always be supplemented by the search for additional contributing perspectives to what is happening, why, and to what effect.

Embedded Values

A fourth characteristic of inquiry processes and products undertaken for education is the unavoidability of values. Neither the concepts, the terms, the methodologies, nor the modes of reporting, disseminating, or utilizing the results can ever be successfully disconnected from or drained of the values embedded in them.[3]

In part this is because of the affective or emotional content of the metaphors we employ. In part it is because of the inevitability that the conceptualizations we employ are devised precisely to understand what is important, for either positive or negative reasons; we cannot avoid the attention thus given and the weighting that comes with it. In part it is because the choices made to adopt conceptualization "x" or employ inquiry methodology "y" or to present to audience "z" require judgments of significance, importance, or at least pertinence (cf. again, the Heather Fairbanks story for illustrations of those choices). Values, in any of the approaches to inquiry for education that might conceivably be employed or any of the formulations of the problems or reasons for undertaking their analysis, simply cannot be avoided. (Some of my colleagues[4] would rightly have me say **valuing** rather than values, thus expressing the active, verb-al, non-attribute but attribut**ed** character of what is being referenced here.)

The only hope, then, since any narrower sense of objectivity is impossible, is to increase consciousness about the values and valuing going on in any given instance of inquiry and to consider what alternative values might well be applied by, perhaps, others who conceivably have a stake in that purpose to which any given specific inquiry might be directed.

(It is important to note that the term value has at least two different meanings. One is merely the expression of interest or perceived worth. The second is the more demanding and powerful sense of imperative, value as "oughtness" implying obligation, either as moral or ethic. Both senses of value are referenced in the discussion above.)

A last point requires mention. Inquiry must be conducted in some context. That context is not a foregone conclusion; the inquirer has real choices. What **is** important, however, is that all inquiry takes place from a vantage point; the acceptance of that operating context is implicitly an alliance with it. To that extent the values resident in that context are served and others not. For example, if I choose to work on curriculum rather than instructional technique I am implicitly valuing content over process. If I choose to work on better understanding the processes of human learning rather than instructional technique I am, in effect, implying that what goes on in the learner is more important than what the teacher does. If I focus on incentives for recruiting "more capable" people to teaching rather than on improvement of the professional training I am allied with the judgment that personal qualities and experience are more valuable than formal training. If I work on an "academic" research problem rather than a development project I am in implicit alliance with the view that it is more important to **know** than to **do.** The choices and the values embedded in them are unavoidable.

Human Consciousness

A fifth characteristic of behavioral and social inquiry is its susceptibility to human consciousness. For example, the mere fact of being studied summons attention and alters perspectives on the object of inquiry. Consciousness over time, especially as it pertains to the history of unfolding events, has the effect of altering the meaning or worth of previously established relationships. A particularly blatant example might be the extent to which psychological testing profiles must be changed because what constitutes normal or abnormal orientations shifts over time (e.g. hair length as a measure of youthful rebelliousness).

The very fact of doing a piece of inquiry alters the nature of the problem being studied. The doing of a piece of inquiry alters the situation, makes it in some sense new, makes it not yet fully known, and by implication never fully knowable. I have vivid memories as a boy of my father commenting on the irony of **TIME**'s cover story devoted to David Riesman's concept of other-directed man. The day the magazine gave popular vent to the concept was the day it no longer bore the same degree of truth that it had the week before it appeared. Each person reading it was certain to respond in one fashion or another. In eliciting such responses Riesman's description and analysis altered what he had just described.

Because of human consciousness, human behavior as an object of inquiry presents something of the characteristic of the no-longer-with-us Old Dutch Cleanser can with its little Dutch girl holding a can of Old Dutch Cleanser with **its** picture of a little Dutch girl holding a can and so on into infinity.

Furthermore, given human consciousness, even the mere examination of an issue can have as much impact as any outcomes of the inquiry. Indeed, non-fruitful inquiries can have as much effect as successful ones, by leading to withdrawal of support for or interest in further study that might be more productive. Conversely, it is also possible to demonstrate that highly successful instances of inquiry can be equally problematical for the prospect of future work. Prime instances exist in the field of curriculum development, for example, the much (and very unfairly) maligned Man: A Course of Study and present views of the worth of the National Science Foundation curriculum improvement initiatives of the 1950's and 60's.

The generic way human consciousness works on inquiry, of course, is through the interaction effect referenced above. There is also a relationship between the effects of human consciousness and the characteristic value-embeddedness of behavioral and social inquiry. If the very act of inquiry has the capacity to alter situations studied, it is to that extent an intervention in the social process. Interventions in the social process are always at some level (because of the values dimension) political acts for which others can expect to hold the inquirers accountable.

IMPLICATIONS FOR INQUIRY IN SUPPORT OF EDUCATION

There are several secondary implications of the characteristics addressed above. Some have already been mentioned, for example, the accountability of social and behavioral inquirers for the interventions their inquiry constitutes, the effects of time, history, and human consciousness on the stability or immutability of the phenomena being studied, and the likelihood, therefore, that the phenomena giving rise to the inquiry can ever be thoroughly understood. There are others.

Non-Cumulative Character

Popular conceptions of science hold that, when it is done properly, it will have a cumulative character. While scholars of science would quarrel some with that view in the larger scheme of things, it has nonetheless -- and especially in the shorter run of things -- a certain amount of truth to it.

But is the hoped-for cumulative character of inquiry in the natural sciences possible in behavioral and social inquiry? Increasingly scholars doubt that it is.[5] Instead, what we can hope to accomplish is to illuminate the present, identifying extant characteristics and their relationships to one another.[6]

Illumination is by no means either a simple or less important aim, especially in the context of an enterprise so deeply affected by valuational considerations and the metaphorical character of description and explanation. Values are diverse; the richness of metaphorical interpretations of social reality matches the plurality of world views, perspectives, and purposes in a free society such as ours. The implications seem clear; behavioral and social inquiry in support of education must reflect the desirability, indeed, the **need**, to support and sustain work that systematically affords opportunity for reflectiveness serving **more** than one perspective.

Is the Academic Search for Generalization Justified?

Much of the inquiry done in support of education and instruction has sought to establish generalizations on the basis of which laws and theories (the latter referring to explanations, **not** mere hypotheses) can be defined. Given that the temporal, value-embedded, metaphorical, and susceptible-to-human-consciousness character of behavioral and social inquiry is correct, then the implication is pretty clear that the search for generalization may be misplaced. The aim to "illuminate," a word used before in this essay, may be more appropriate. The particular metaphor "illuminate," however, suggests much -- for example, from different angles, with different intensity, directly, indirectly, through screens or gels (not to push the metaphor further, perhaps, than one should).

While this implication has much to say to academic inquiry and scholarship in support of education, it has bearing on practice, too; scholarly understandings shape the conceptual context from which practitioners undertake their daily responsibilities. But it also suggests the caution that those engaging in and using practice-oriented inquiry should exhibit in contemplating the design of evaluation studies, for example, that might conceivably be used to guide practice in other settings, or in applying a strategy today devised for a situation assessed yesterday.

Different Epistemologies

Epistemology is the study of knowledge -- what it is, how it is acquired, and so on. One of its central concerns, for example, is attention to what it means to claim that something is "known,""true," or empirically valid.

If what has been said so far in this chapter is accurate, then in "knowing" things about learning, schooling, and education it is almost certainly true that different epistemologies will be encountered. There is, in short, no "Greenwich mean standard" of knowledge. Instead, there are competing, maybe conflicting, but in any case different standards of equal validity and importance.

Let me suggest three -- the standard applied by the academic community, the standard applied by practitioners, and the standards applied by those who seek the benefits of learning from society's formal institutions and arrangements for education. (I do not mean to suggest that there are only three or that there will not be considerable variation within the three main categories; there will. Referencing three categories, however, should make it possible to establish the point.)

Scholars view the world they look at from the perspective of their academic disciplines. The inquiry they engage in aims to further the understanding of reality from that perspective, with all the attendant values, metaphors, and methodological controls that enable them to achieve their ends. The story opening the chapter, however, suggests that the "purity" of view some might otherwise ascribe to a discipline-based perspective is not immune from the effects of self-interest or special context, even if responsibly treated.

Practitioners do not have the same perspective nor can they afford the luxury of control. Instead, they must work in a world of multiple variables and complex interactions that grossly exceed those willingly encompassed by scholars. They cannot afford the privilege of being able to carefully define, delimit, and and otherwise "hold still" what is happening purely in order to understand. Practitioners have purposes to achieve for others. They ride a rapidly changing wave, having to respond to emergent conditions, frequently, with great swiftness.

The lessened ability of practitioners to control the variables to which they are subject does not mean that practitioners are necessarily at a disadvantage, or, conversely, that what scholars can establish is necessarily likely to have greater power or truth because of the advantages under which they operate. The experience of and approach to reality is different; neither is superior to the other. Scholars have certain capabilities and prerogatives which are helpful to them. On the other hand, practitioners handle, minute by minute, numbers of variables in complex relation to one another, orders of magnitude greater than that of even the most sophisticated formal studies. The demands of practice and the rapidity with which events there take place, however, make it likely that much that might productively be approached at a conscious level cannot begin to be so accessed.

Many analogous things can be said about those who would be **served** by schools and education, and about those, principally legislators and other policy makers, who represent the interests of those seeking or needing to be served. The clients' perceptions of "knowing" have to do with the benefits they (or their guardians) anticipate getting from their schooling. They are concerned with the meaning of what is happening to and for them and how that relates to aspirations or expectations of their engagement with the real world. Again, as in the case of comparisons between scholars' and practitioners' views of reality, the clients' views cannot be placed in rank order relative to the other two. They, too, are different, possessing a power, vitality, and validity all their own.

The implications of this understanding about the diversity of epistemologies for educational inquiry speak, again, to the complexity of the situation.[7] The implications, however, are mainly the burden of scholars and practitioners, since it is they who are charged with acting on the basis of understandings that can be warranted. The clients of educational institutions and practice ought not to be expected, necessarily, either to understand such matters or, indeed, to be aware of them. Coping with what it means to know know is the responsibility of practitioners and those others in the academic and research communities who provide them with essential support through inquiry.

CHAPTER SEVEN

HOW CAN FORMAL INQUIRY PROCESSES AND
PRODUCTS COME TO IMPROVE EDUCATION?

Chapter Four offered a number of specific examples of inquiry processes and products applied to the field of education. Chapters Five and Six categorized and characterized inquiry analytically and descriptively. The present chapter seeks to approach the topic in still a third way by addressing the connections between formal inquiry and educational practice.

The professional literature, particularly in the research and development sector, contains a fair amount of material on the relationship of research to practice. Some of it has been theoretical and reflective in character, exploring logically and systematically how the two relate. The larger portion, particularly in recent years, has focussed, in part analytically but increasingly from a research orientation itself, on so-called change processes in education. Until very recently the operating assumptions guiding this literature reflected the belief that knowledge has typically emerged at some distance from practice and that the "puzzle" lay in causing practice to be better informed by what was known. In the past several years, more change process research has been conducted. Recognition of the special characteristics of behavioral and social knowledge has become more widespread. One result, for example, may be seen in the increasing attention given to engaging practitioner communities directly in inquiry processes as a way of stimulating and defining knowledge-based change in education.

MODELS OF THE RELATION OF RESEARCH AND DEVELOPMENT TO EDUCATIONAL PRACTICE

The literature on the relationship of formal inquiry to the improvement of practice can perhaps be introduced most usefully by noting at the outset the extent to which it reflects one of the central conclusions of the previous chapter. Behavioral and social inquiry contributes multiple perspectives on what is happening in learning, in classrooms, in schools, and in universities. The concept of multiple perspectives is fully reflected in the literature on the relationship of inquiry to practice. Consider the diversity of the views abstracted below.

Systems Schema

An early representation of the relation of research to practice defined logically the relationship of the categories of research, development, dissemination, and utilization.[1] Such schemas present the goal of educational improvement as being dependent upon adequate diffusion mechanisms which in turn require the design and development of tested innovations to diffuse, which in turn depend upon the adequacy of the knowledge base generated from research. Thus, the theoretical continuum from research to practice begins with research. Development, the next stage, consists of invention and design. The dissemination stage includes demonstration activities as well as more traditional information distribution. Adoption, the final stage in this kind of schema, also has component elements -- trial, installation and institutionalization.

Decision Models

A contrasting view to the systems schema focusses more on the discontinuities between the different types of activity encompassed under the heading "inquiry for education."[2] These models draw attention to the different rules of evidence and sources and types of data input for decision-making in each activity. While the relationships among the activities are recognized, decision models tend to focus on the decisionmaking requirements at the time of decision rather than on patterns and relationships which may emerge by logical analysis or as a result of historical analysis of change.

Market Model

Developed originally as a debate-generating alternative to the systems schema, a fourth model focused attention not on the research end of the logical spectrum but on the practice end.[3] Even it presumed, to a certain extent, the logical if not the practical primacy of scholarly research. This conceptualization based on an insight of Theodore Leavitt touted the worth of the "market" -- that is, teachers, administrators, and others -- coming to define its practitioner needs for more effective instructional resources through the initiation of far more extensive evaluation activities. The results of that evaluation would then, in effect, form the agenda for the bulk of the work undertaken by an expanded research and development sector.

Linkage Models

Linkage models stress the close interrelations of research, development, and dissemination, or, conversely, the need to perform functions between them.[4] Some models in this category have a tendency to be performer-oriented (that is, performers of formal inquiry) and to stress the importance of individuals in a research-development-dissemination continuum. Some stress the linkage between research and development which is seen to be bi-directional. Research is seen as sometimes leading to the suggestion for the development of new techniques; sometimes development suggests new kinds of research problems or issues. Still other linkage models focus heavily on what might be called brokerage functions between inquiry activities and categories, especially between the development of validated innovations and their adoption in other sites.

Configurational Model

The configurational view of educational research and development was developed because of perceived weaknesses in the systems view, particularly the extent to which the logical model displayed significant discrepancies from the real institutional world of research and development for education.[5] The configurational view describes a community-like model of the domain of educational knowledge production and utilization. The variety of institutions and individuals in the domain, it was felt, were far more likely to view themselves as related to one another in a community sense than in an organizational sense. It defined the educational knowledge production and utilization domain as the full range of operating educational agencies or institutions in the country.

Legitimization of Practice

This view of the relationship of research to practice neatly reverses the logic of the systems view.[6] It stresses the critical role played by research is the legitimization of practice. In this conception practice is perceived as often preceding theory or, at least, formal verification. The inventive practitioner mind develops ideas and techniques later validated by the work of formal research or evaluation.

Adaptation Models

Recent evaluation and change process research has led to the articulation of what might be called adaptation models of the relation of research to practice.[7] Here the realities of practitioner commitment, experience, and knowledge, together with the requirements of institutional change, are seen as virtually assuring that research-based change, whether conceptual or developmental in character, will go through some kind of adaptation in the local site. Much of the success of that process is seen as having something to do with opportunities for professional staff truly to make innovations their own through participation in the adaptation process.

DISCUSSION

There may well be other models. Those presented above are more than sufficient to make the point; there are many views of the relationship of inquiry to practice. Given their premises, all of the models make sense, although it should be clear that not all of them can be employed simultaneously. Each embodies a particular view of the institutional or epistemological world in education. Each expresses priorities relative to the importance of one or another dimension, category, function or purpose of inquiry processes and products for education. Each fits a particular set of values and a particular view of the role of teachers, scholars, innovators, and clients of educational institutions.

The importance of being clear on R&D models lies in the extent to which the "vantage point" adopted by inquirers on such matters constitutes, as suggested in the preceding chapter, that with which they are in alliance. Further, to the extent that there are unresolved differences or conflicts of view, impediments to fruitful interchange or relation may exist. How we see the products of inquiry -- academic or practitioner oriented, formal or casual -- fitting into the larger scheme of knowledge creation and utilization, will affect how it is initiated and undertaken, with whom, what criteria are applied in its conception, development, and implementation, and what is done with the results. In short, whether we are explicit about such notions or carry them around with us only at an unconscious, implicit level, they will constitute important shaping influences to what we do, how, and with what effect.

Part Three

**FROM CONCEPT TO ACTION
(or, THEORY TO PRACTICE!)**

CHAPTER EIGHT   **PREFACE TO ACTION**

TWO ASSUMPTIONS

The foregoing chapters have sought to provide and analyze numerous concrete illustrations of inquiry processes and products applied to education. They have sought to suggest how the adoption of a comprehensive inquiry frame of mind applied to all aspects of the educational system might constitute a far-reaching and productive break with the past. Illustrations and suggestions, however, are not necessarily guides to action.

The present chapter introduces the bulk of the remainder of the essay. It is based on a pair of assumptions. The first is that what has been said so far is reasonably accurate. In the context of a proposal as broad as this one and as projective in its orientation, accuracy must be thought of in two ways. Is it descriptively accurate based on past experience? Would academics, researchers, teacher educators, teachers, educational administrators, and policy officials recognize and attest to what has been said? The second test focuses on the legitimacy of the proposition advanced in terms of its perceived value acted upon in the future. Does the argument hold? If educators, in all their many roles and inter-linked responsibilities, began now to move in the directions suggested, would the benefits claimed be likely to emerge over the next several decades?

The second assumption on which Part Two rests is that, after completing Part One, the reader believes (or at least is willing to continue entertaining the belief) that fundamentally re-thinking the profession of education on the organizing principle of inquiry broadly defined is worth undertaking.

THE PURPOSES AND PLAN OF THE MEMORANDUM APPROACH

Connections between ideas and action are only rarely obvious and immediate. To draw them takes time, effort, and at least some imagination. Furthermore, to devise an action plan for a domain as diverse and as large as education requires attention to a very large number of roles. Complicating matters still further, the organizational "plan" for education affords great amounts of policy and professional latitude to most of the roleplayers.

Who Are the Roleplayers? How Were They Chosen? The Memoranda in Part Two are directed to sixteen such roleplayers. Some of the roleplayers are singular, for example, the Director of the National Institute of Education or the Executive Director of the American Association of Colleges for Teacher Education. Some memos are aimed at a class of officials, for example, the governors of the fifty States or Chief State School Officers, limited in number though certainly not in power, as recent widely reported events have shown.

Others, like the memos directed to practitioner-based or stakeholder organizations, aim at literally thousands of people. The roleplayers addressed in this essay do not exhaust the list that might be devised, but they certainly illustrate the range and suggest the complexity of the task.

The memoranda directed to singular roleplayers should **not** be read as being directed to the individual currently performing the indicated responsibilities. To have crafted them in that way might have been tempting in the interests of immediate action, but doing so could also have led to unnecessary or unuseful personalizing, distracting attention from the generic tasks. From a pragmatic perspective, too -- and this is certainly one of the troublesome dimensions of engendering purposive action for the profession -- the turnover of personnel in such highly visible posts in positions of public authority is so frequent, that to write to an individual in the context of a published document like this is to risk beaming the message to an empty switchboard! Offering these caveats certainly should not be interpreted as a denial of the crucial difference that individuals can make in the roles they occupy. Personality and persuasion can be of enormous import!

How Complete Are the Prescriptions? The scope of the proposed reconceptualization is such that it is unlikely that one individual could hope to imagine or encompass all the implications for each of the roles examined. In the course of my association with the profession, however, I have encountered either the principal actors or representative figures for all of the roles considered here. Based on that experience the intent behind each memorandum is to identify an illustrative if not exhaustive set of implications based on the notions expressed in the preceding chapters. I simply placed myself in each role and tried to imagine what might be required of an understanding of Parts One and Two of this essay and hypothetical agreement with its aims.

Such an exercise is fraught with potential disaster. It is possible that roles are misconceived. It is possible that the translation between concept and role is inaccurately constructed. That covers but two; there are, no doubt, more.

It seems worthwhile taking the risk, however. If the conception advanced has merit and the contents of the memoranda are flawed, someone will surely come forward with corrections. If there are possible actions that have not been identified, others may be able to supplement. Of greater importance than being right or complete is to make the attempt, to illustrate how hundreds of key officials and thousands of professionals, working with thousands of laypersons might be able to achieve improvement in the Nation's educational systems through the fundamental reconceptualization proposed here.

MEMO ONE

To: America's Teachers and Principals

I imagine some of you are surprised on at least three different levels. He's addressing us **first**! He's addressing us **together**! And after reading the preceding pages he's addressing us **at all**!

The fact remains that unless a significant portion of the profession and its leadership come to believe a proposal like this has merit, it will never happen. It is equally true, however, that individually, as teachers and principals, there may not seem to be much that each of you can do to move the larger enterprise in the directions suggested. In fact, I wouldn't be a bit surprised that at this point any principals reading this memo might be doing so with understandable skepticism after having read some of the things written in Chapter Three.

I would say, first, then, to both teachers and principals, that the proposal advanced here is not going to jeopardize anyone's immediate job anytime soon. The proposal is clearly a long-range one. Like all long-range proposals there will be ample time for individuals to adjust or maybe even to ride things out to the conclusion of their present careers working effectively, given present frames of reference, performing valuable and valued services. The changes projected in the proposal advanced in these pages are substantial, and they will come about only incrementally in the system as a whole. They will **not** come about incrementally in individual buildings, I would guess. The change-overs contemplated, however, will be some time in coming.

Models of schools operated in this way will need to be designed and tested.[1] Eventual reform will proceed on a building by building basis, with very little progress to show in the early years, a steady shift in the intervening decade and a half, and the slow-down as the entire nation moves in that direction. If a chart of that progress were to be drawn it might look like a giant rectangle on its side with a sweeping S-curve starting in the lower left hand corner lifting up to a steady thirty-degree angle for most of the distance and then "saturating" to the upper right hand corner, the entire progress of the line spanning three or four decades. No one should feel his or her role is immediately threatened by the proposal advanced here. The first thing to do in contributing to the advance proposed here, therefore, is **not worry** excessively about its immediate implications.

The second thing to do is **think about it.** In many respects nothing I have said here should startle any reflective teacher or principal. "Of course that's what we try to do every day, every moment. We're always asking questions -- when we can. We always try to act on what we know -- if we have time to think about it. We've always known of the importance of reliance upon our peers for insights and help -- when we can summon the energy and create the opportunity after the working day." But **think** about it again. If inquiry is powerful and could support your daily behavior, if knowing more conceptually and practically could benefit you, then what stands (or stood) in the way of realizing that benefit? Being clear about such matters is the first step to setting the professional agenda in your school or district.

That leads to the third step you can take as front-line professionals. Based on the agenda, begin to ask for the removal of the impediments and for the support you need to ask and answer the questions that arise in your daily work. As teachers, your quest may be directed to your principals or superintendents, your school boards, the teacher training institutions you work with (or went to -- they are becoming increasingly attentive to the messages from their graduates), or authorities at the state level.

The reflectiveness about the performance of your own responsibilities may not prove easy or always painless. Questions that might help you in your explorations might include:

1. What do I know that is powerful in carrying out my responsibilities? Can I identify gaps in my background knowledge or the data on the immediate in-structional situation facing me?

2. What kinds of inquiry **do** I engage in? What are my strategies for undertaking it?

3. What do I do when I realize I don't know what I need to? How do I recognize I'm at that point? How do I move past that point? (These last questions come from a point of view that says that one way professionals demonstrate their competence is what they do in situations when they don't know what to do, recognize that fact, and take responsible actions nonetheless. So much for teacher or administrator competencies narrowly defined!)

4. What help is available to me?

5. What information, materials, and other resources should the system be providing to me **now** that would enable me to act professionally on what I **know** now? Have I asked for those resources (either individually or collectively) with a well-grounded rationale based on state-of-the-art understandings of curriculum, instruction, multi-factored assessment of student achievement, and so on?

6. How do I know that what I am doing is effective? What kinds of information ought I to be able to collect or otherwise have made available to me that would assist me in maintaining and improving the level of my performance in my responsibilities?

These questions are illustrative. The list could be easily expanded. The point is to stimulate reflectiveness about the definition of professional role advanced. To the extent that such reflectiveness is widely stimulated across the Nation's schools and colleges it will become essential pressure for movement in the directions proposed.

Finally, a suggestion to "the organized profession," the members and officers of the NEA and AFT. Until teachers speak with one voice, achieving any kind of professional reform across the Nation will be difficult. Recent experience of the ease with which political figures used the current bifurcation to political (but certainly not educational) advantage speaks to the long-range desirability of taking a page from the histories of the American Federation of Labor and the Congress of Industrial Organizations and begin to work **now** toward a future ten years from now when a new professional organization, the NFEAT (the National Federation of Educators and Teachers), emerges on the national scene. A ten year project could permit the making of all the adjustments in staff offices at State and national levels, provide for an orderly transition, resolve the current anomaly of only the NEA being represented on the national accrediting body for teacher education, and establish a unified force for teachers' professional identity and development. The principal value to the reconceptualization advanced here would be the substantial reduction of energies now allocated to the politics of competition and division, energy that could, instead, be directed to what Gary Sykes calls education's "professional project."[2]

MEMO TWO

To: Governors of the Fifty States

Events of recent weeks and months have thrust you into a crucial position in the reformation of American education. With vigorous gubernatorial leadership several states have launched sweeping programs to change the approaches currently being taken in finance, teacher recruitment and training, compensation, length of the school year, and so on. It is fair to say that eighteen months ago few would have predicted the depth of the public demand for action, the speed with which steps are being taken, or the extent of the involvement of political leadership at the highest levels in States all across the nation. The recent Portland, Maine, Governors' Conference afforded ample evidence of the deep interest and intention to act in many quarters.[1]

Education may be the most important single responsibility of State governments. What the States do has consequences within and far beyond their own borders. But education is also a long-range enterprise. Few can hope in their tenure as Governor to see the results of their efforts, let alone reap the benefits, for they take years to achieve. The temptation, therefore, to work on taxes, highways, economic development, or prisons, to name just a few alternatives, is great, because the results will be visible within reasonable spans of time. Not so education. Perhaps even less so the proposal advanced in Part One of this essay. But it is not necessary to endorse the entire conception sketched out there. It is only necessary to agree that teachers, administrators, and teacher educators be held to the aspirations of acting on the basis of what is known, that they understand how and why those things are known, and that they approach their daily work with the unalterable commitment to engage in inquiry appropriate to their professional roles, whatever they might be and wherever necessary, to sustain and enhance the partnerships required for effective schooling to occur. That is a worthy goal for the public **and** the profession, and it is one that can be pressed from the highest political office in each State.

All of education has to be gratified with the fact of the political leadership emerging at the State level even if we cannot agree with some of the specifics that have been offered from time to time. The leadership forthcoming from the Federal level has been almost exclusively hortatory, not bad in itself, but no substitute, either, for the initiatives that must eventually be forthcoming. Action at the State level is essential; that is the way America is politically organized for educational purposes. The vigorous involvement of governors, therefore, is crucial. If you see this proposal as contributing to a grounding of the profession and system of education, what role could you play, in effect, to prevent in the future the kind of twenty year cycle of attention that seems to characterize America's interest in education?

You are no strangers to the complexity of the educational enterprise in each of your States. Your role is certainly affected by the existence of a State Board of Education (or equivalent body) and a Chief State School Officer, either or both of which may be appointed or elected. There is a large administrative bureaucracy at the State level over which you have little direct authority, and you work with a legislature whose ways, in every State and often for very good reasons, are sometimes wondrous to behold.

If you found yourself persuaded by the prospective benefits of the profession of education and the institutions of schooling moving in the directions proposed, if you found the organizing principle of inquiry a powerful one, what aims might you seek to serve? I would urge three on you. First, keep the heat on the education establishment through your leadership. Second, wherever possible insist upon comprehensiveness and simplicity in the rationale underpinning forthcoming proposals for reform. Third, use your good offices as well as any real authority you may have, to highlight the importance of the relationship between higher education and lower education in effecting desired changes.

LEADERSHIP

Where State education officials are elected they are likely to appreciate the need to be directly responsive to public unhappiness over the schools. The profession, however, and I include in that designation its elected, appointed, and civil service membership, has a way of getting immersed in the complexities of its own intricate relationships, sometimes ignoring the immediate reality and validity of the public's concern. Keeping an eye and a spotlight on that (whenever needed) is an important function. Governors command attention in officialdom and the media. When the claims on educators are framed in terms of goals they all agree with and to which they ought to be held accountable, leadership from the Governor can have direct professional effect as well.

Be cautious, however, about how you respond to the numerous reports and recommendations that have and will surface this year. For example, the economy is important, but, in America, the polity is even more so. If America's schools and colleges meet the basic interests of the latter, the interests of the former will be served as well. Be careful, too, about the implications of the specific recommendations advanced. For example, A Nation At Risk advocated a longer school day and longer year, but the research evidence more clearly suggests better use can be made of the time currently available to us and the thoughtful exposition of Ernest Boyer actually makes recommendations that would require a lessening of the direct instructional responsibilities of teachers in the interests of better planning and more responsive evaluation of student work.

RATIONALES

Asking "how" and "why" at the highest level of State government, therefore, seems an especially legitimate form of activity even where the authority of the education establishment is virtually independent of State executive authority. Budgets have to be presented to legislatures, the overall level of State financial effort assayed, the relationship of educational productivity to economic health and development calculated, and relative shares of State wealth to competing claims adjudicated. Wherever efficiency and effectiveness of a central State responsibility can be improved is a matter with a claim on gubernatorial attention.

In a sense what is being argued is another way of pressing for heightened standards of performance by the system. A good starting point is with the quality of the argumentation on the basis of which reforms are proposed and justified. A negative example can be given. In several states proposals have been written into law or regulation which will have the effect of opening the ranks of teaching to individuals who will have had little or no exposure to knowledge, conceptual or practical, essential for effective performance in schools and classrooms. In the shortrun that is likely to have little effect on the schools; in the long run it is likely to increase public unhappiness if they see little result from the reform or, worse, as its effects are the reverse of those intended as untrained persons quickly leave thereby increasing turnover and instability in the schools or, bluntly, they screw up because they don't know what they ought to. Earlier in this essay I cited Mencken's caution against simple, obvious solutions to social problems. Opening classrooms to untrained individuals is an example. Others could be given. One way to help prevent such mistakes is to require the entire system to act on knowledge instead of mere belief or opinion by demanding thoughtful rationales and closely reasoned, long-range policy analysis.

BETTER RELATING HIGHER AND LOWER EDUCATION TO ONE ANOTHER

The responsibilities of higher education relative to an educational system that functions on the basis of knowledge and inquiry (as contrasted to habit, tradition, or inertia) are very substantial and seriously under-considered. In most of your States the executive establishments for the two systems are separate and distinct. While there may be a great deal of coordination between the two (recently around admissions requirements to higher education, for example) and while the agency responsible for lower education has coordinate responsibility in most instances because of its teacher certification authority, it remains the case that higher education has not given the attention to professional training in education that it ought to have.

There are at least three dimensions of this:

1. Institutions and State subvention formulae undersupport teacher education.

2. Public and private institutions of higher education have allowed attention to their responsibilities for general or liberal education to languish in the face of competing professional orientations of the academic disciplines themselves.

3. The quality and character of far too much teaching in higher education affords beginning teachers poor models of what they themselves are being asked to learn and apply in the schools where they will teach.

The circumstances described above for teacher education characterize most states. They have existed for a long time and for a complex set of reasons that will not yield to short-term efforts. Your position as governor midway between the higher education establishment and that responsible for lower education gives you a unique opportunity. I would urge you to start by convening the heads of teacher education, college and university presidents, academic vice presidents, the leadership of the organized teachers in the state, and the State education authorities responsible for teacher certification in a carefully orchestrated working conference. Its purpose would be to consider the teacher education picture in your state in light of the implications of improving effective service in education by increasing attention to its knowledge base and the importance of inquiry processes throughout the profession.

More specifically, the focus of the conference ought to be to undertake needed dialogue on the knowledge base for teacher education, the prospects of it being passed on adequately in the four year program, the recruitment of more highly qualified teacher education candidates, achieving an adequate allocation of resources to teacher education, the admittedly difficult problem of the shortcomings present in the models and quality of instruction currently offered in higher education, and the implications of a forthcoming professional teaching role increasingly characterized by forms of practical inquiry. The prestige of the Governor's Office would bring the meeting off; careful planning and organization could make such a gathering highly effective.

* * *

These recommendations and observations are highly specific and quite general. As is the case in the other memoranda they are intended to be illustrative only. Different States have different needs and different traditions. Perhaps most important, however, may simply be the recognition that the thrust of this essay represents directions the profession has to assume responsibility for taking, and that the role of political leadership is to encourage such growth and, at least, to act in ways that do not prevent the emergence of a professional frame of mind oriented to knowledge and inquiry processes systematically applied.

MEMO THREE

To: Chief State School Officers

No figure is more central to the educational reform movement than each of you. Mindful of the intensely political nature of your responsibilities and day-to-day activities whether you are elected or appointed, you remain the official in each State with the range of responsibility and the coordinative authority to exercise the kind of leadership required to act to end, once and for all, the cyclical character of America's interest and attention to education.

Part One of this essay proposed a long-range orientation to the improvement of education's capacity to serve the Nation by increasing our grounding on knowledge and practice-based inquiry. It sees, as a consequence, the **creation** of a profession where one does not now exist. There are steps that can begin to be taken now to help move in the directions indicated.

CERTIFICATION STANDARDS

A most direct route, although by no means an easy one, is to carefully examine and re-draw certification packages on the bases of the extant knowledge base for teaching, the assumption of its continuous development, and the definition of the practitioner roles as requiring the ability to engage individually and with others in practice-based, practice-directed inquiry. This would mean, among other things, including in certification guidelines requirements that practitioners be trained in practice-based inquiry skills (especially diagnostics and instructional evaluation), development of collaborative skills, defining permanent certificates in terms that made it clear there would be expectations for periodic endorsements, as well as insistence that certificates could be awarded only for work undertaken in approved programs, not through the presentation of credits accumulated in helter-skelter fashion.

PROGRAM APPROVAL

Virtually all States follow some form of program or institutional approval for offering teacher education programs (here "teacher education" refers broadly to all certifications in education). The process followed to make such evaluations and the criteria employed can be powerful policy tools. For example, colleges and universities can be asked to develop not only descriptions of what they are prepared to offer in the professional preparation programs but **justifications** as well, justifications that are keyed to the knowledge base and the emerging role of practitioner as inquirer.[1]

Of critical importance in evaluating certification programs for approval purposes is the adequacy of the intellectual resources, in quantitative as well as qualitative terms. Do the numbers and kinds of faculty available to offer the certification programs fully reflect the expertise required?

While difficult to assess without intensive site visitation, of critical importance in the training of teachers is the extent to which their own instruction, in the professional preparation offerings as well as the academic content and liberal/general education offerings, is offered in ways which model excellence. Attending to this concern may well generate some negative reaction owing to misplaced concerns about "invasions of domains protected by academic freedom." In the interest of improvement, however, effective teaching models in higher education should be addressed, tactfully and with understanding, but head on.

TESTING TEACHERS

All prospective teachers ought to be tested before being certified. Doing so is a direct extension of the argument that professional practice ought to rest on the appropriate knowledge bases. As a minimum such testing should address basic skills, subject matter mastery, and general knowledge. It should also address pedagogical knowledge, but care should be taken that the desired professional role is the one reflected in the examination. If the professional portion of the available tests assume teaching is "rule applying" behavior, for example, then it will tend to slight the essential practice-based inquiry skills required of the model advanced in this essay.

There is one important corollary of the desirability of testing teachers. If teacher candidates are to be tested, then **the practice of granting temporary certificates ought to be suspended immediately.** The rationale is straight forward: if the knowledge of prospective teachers is important enough to measure before certification, surely no one other than someone possessing such knowledge ought to be admitted to classroom practice.

The pressures on State authorities from local school districts for temporary certificates is very great. On the other hand, tightening up the standards at one end while pulling the plug at the other makes little sense. Part of the reason there is a district demand for temporary certificates has to do with the difficulty of persuading teachers to work for the salaries currently offered. Part has to do with lukewarm recruitment efforts. Part has to do with the understandable desire of districts to keep teachers they would otherwise have to release. Part, however, also has to do with remaining vestiges of chronyism and favoritism on the local scene. Whatever the reasons, granting temporary certificates is retrograde movement. There is a solution, however.

State superintendents could create small cadres of teachers hired at the State level on three-year contracts in those areas where temporary certificates were in special demand. The incentive for the teachers thus hired would be a substantial salary bonus, say $5-7,000, for being willing to serve on a mobile basis. The incentive for the local district to hire its own eventual certified replacements is that the districts would be required to draw on the State pool **and** pay the full salary of the individual (including the bonus). Teachers hired by the State in any given year as part of the pool but not called upon by local districts, would be made available to any teacher or district in the State requesting their use to help individual teachers by observing, sharing, and consulting on the improvement of teaching. Using the certificated cadre in this fashion would also help orient the profession at large to the real benefits that will arise when teaching settings are structured so as to reduce the isolation which now characterizes them.

ENTRY STANDARDS FOR TEACHING CANDIDATES

Organizing the profession of education systematically on its knowledge base and on inquiry practices will require greater attention to the quality of teacher candidates than has been given heretofore. The relative attractiveness of teaching as a profession is not going to improve dramatically in the short-term future. An important reality was described by Terry Herndon, former executive director of the National Education Association, when he remarked recently that he "would not make an effort to convert anybody to the idea that they ought to be a teacher."[2] Furthermore, whether anyone likes it or not, a delicate balance exists between admissions standards and the very survival of the training resource in education. Budgets are figured in higher education on enrollment and the production of FTE's (fulltime equivalent students), and actions on admission standards that would have the effect of reducing enrollments in teacher education could further reduce instructional resources in higher education at precisely the time when the demands for heightened quality would argue for an **increase**.[3] Precipitous actions on admissions standards could, thus, well have net effects counter to the intended aims.

Coordinating the elevation of admission standards across a state is necessary for another reason as well. Expecting individual institutions to act on their own is unrealistic in all but that small handful of the most prestigious institutions. When single institutions either increase their standards or ask for additional data, e.g., on writing capacity, letters of reference, or evidence of involvement in child or community service activities, prospective students simply take their admissions forms elsewhere.[4]

TEACHER EDUCATION AS A POST-BACCALAUREATE ENTERPRISE

Teacher education will become a post-baccalaureate enterprise in the foreseeable future. The reason is to be found in the demands of the knowledge base and the need to insist on the foundations of general knowledge and content mastery. Further, admitting students with the bachelor's degree gives great promise of being the vehicle by which the elevated admissions standards can be achieved. While it may be too early to begin planning for that, you should be aware of the prospect and begin reflecting on its implications and requirements.

STANDARDS FOR ELEMENTARY AND SECONDARY SCHOOLS

The need to rethink the structure of schools along the lines suggested in Part One makes examination of State standards a logical activity for you to initiate. Ultimately, the entire structure of schooling will require examination, but a short-term activity would be to review standards that support or impede the opportunity of teachers to work directly with one another during the working day and to spend time on the classroom-based operations research (practice-based inquiry) activities that assure maintenance and enhancement of quality. In the long run, however, the extent to which school standards embrace differentiated roles, salaries, and certification will require examination.

COPING WITH DEMANDS FOR LOCAL AUTONOMY

The proposals advanced in the essay, as suggested in several of these memoranda, raise anew old issues of autonomy in various parts of the Nation's educational systems. School districts are understandably jealous of their prerogatives. Colleges and universities (to say nothing of individual faculty therein) defend vigorously their rights to decide on curriculum and instructional matters. The creation of a true profession in education will reinforce (if not create) legitimate claims for teacher autonomy to decide how to approach curricular and instructional matters in the context of district goals and the teachers' increased access to knowledge and data growing from the application of practice-directed inquiry.

These will not be easy claims to resolve. All of them have value, but together they have the potential for conflict. School districts have the authority to choose less effective instructional models, but can the State afford the long-term results? Extremely important traditions of academic freedom, essential to the pursuit and dissemination of knowledge, may appear to conflict with legitimate claims for accountability or the maintenance of standards. Claims for professional autonomy necessarily rest on professional expertise, but the potential for real or apparent conflict with goals and objectives defined by local authorities always exists. More effective schools occasioned by more systematic attention to inquiry processes and knowledge, will exacerbate these conflicts rather than resolve them. State education authorities will need to anticipate such conflicts and devise strategies for resolving them.

LEADERSHIP FOR THE PROFESSION

This memo started out acknowledging the intensity of your political environment. Regardless of the particular nature of the issues confronting you at any given point in time, the aims suggested by this essay's frame of reference are uniquely yours to serve. That uniqueness is a function of your leadership role. You serve in a position from which a unified profession of education could finally be formed out of the disparate elements now tugging in so many different directions.

Unification will not be achieved by directive, of course, but the powers of persuasion exercised in the interest of professional leadership can be considerable. Your responsibilities for teacher education and certification give you necessary links to higher education. Your responsibilities for finance give you access, at least, to levers whereby the system can be moved. Your relationship to the Governor and the legislature affords you opportunities to describe and justify the importance of knowledge and inquiry as grounds for professional practice. Your role in the formulation and enforcement of standards, present and prospective, is central. Your relationships with practitioner-based organizations, PTA's, and representatives of the organized profession put you near the middle of the continuous flow of interest groups on matters of educational policy and practice in your State. No single figure in education (and only the Governor outside) has the same reach or capacity for effective action. If grounding professional practice on knowledge and inquiry processes makes sense to you in the long haul, then I urge on you the beginning steps suggested here.

MEMO FOUR

To: My Fellow Heads of Teacher Education

As the professional leaders administratively responsible for the initial (and a very large portion of the continuing) preparation of teachers and other education practitioners and administrators, our help in grounding the profession on the processes and products of inquiry will be crucial. We have much to do.

PROFESSIONAL CURRICULA

While we operate in the context of certification outlines, program standards, and accreditation guidelines, a great deal of latitude exists within our institutions, especially as regards assuring that our programs adequately reflect the current state of underpinning knowledge. The curricular content of our professional preparation programs ought to contain the product of past inquiry and fully reflect the insights of reflective scholarship. Furthermore, given the thrust of the recommendations contained in this essay, teacher education programs should also come to grips with the centrality of practice-based inquiry processes to the successful performance of the newly defined teaching role. Calling for these ends is easy; accomplishing them is less so.

Imagine a blank, white wall being made available for each of your professional preparation programs and a supply of felt-tip pens of three colors. On the wall is to be written all of the elements of the professional curriculum. By element is meant the very specific content to be covered and the manner in which it is to be covered. The program goals are **not** to be written on the wall; they would be somewhere else on the side. Using a different color for each type of entry, the aim of the exercise is to write the content elements down, **together with two different justifying statements**. The first justifying statement would key the element to the program goal(s) that it serves. The second justifying statement would establish the warrant for its inclusion as "knowledge"; it would address on what basis the element's inclusion had been established by formal inquiry or scholarship. Before any curricular element would be allowed to stay on the wall it would have to be justified by the two key statements. This process has one additional implication worth mentioning. Once an item gets on the wall, what is the justification for removing it? The redevelopment of the "white wall" over time holds the prospect of helping avoid the over-responsiveness of American education to fad and fashion.

There are two process benefits of the "white wall" technique. First, it enables the exercise to be a collaborative one. The ability of many participants simultaneously to see entries allows a group of individuals to work together from their diverse perspectives. Second, the technique also enables the participants to maintain a sense of the whole as they work together.

Completing an exercise of this kind will force examination of the extent to which we are capable as a profession of establishing and articulating the epistemological justifications for what we include in our curricula. Identifying a line of research for a firmly established concept is one thing. Distinguishing it from beliefs, personal experiences, a value position, or an hypothesis (no matter how logical) is another. To the extent that we employ any of these other justifications we have far less of a claim to professional status for ourselves and our profession. Claims of professional standing tend to "stick" only where an esoteric body of knowledge can be identified, justified, and in the long run demonstrated to be of instrumental value in the achievement of the aims of that profession. This kind of exercise should improve preparation curricula even as it will help to secure the basis for teacher education's claims to expertise.

CLIMATE FOR INQUIRY

The profession itself cannot hope to develop a commitment to inquiry if schools and colleges of education do not display such commitments as well. That does **not** mean that every school of education has to have a fullscale research and development effort. It does mean a commitment to curricular currency and the presence of the same kinds of practice-based and practice-directed inquiry we would hope practitioners in the schools could conduct. Are we monitoring our curricular effectiveness? Do we, in fact, adopt the multiple perspectives of behavioral and social inquiry to guide both curriculum and instruction within our professional preparation programs? Sustaining such traditions where they exist and enhancing them in the far more numerous instances where they do not is a task for us to undertake.

Certainly an important matter in establishing a climate for inquiry is considering how the faculty of a department, school, or college of education understand their epistemological roots. As an old foundations person I might be tempted to turn them all into philosophers, but that is not what I mean here. I mean to ask how conscious we are about the bases for the content we teach, the prescriptions we offer to the schools, and the empirical or logical ground for the professional positions we espouse. A critical frame of mind is vital for any institution of higher education aiming to establish the profession of education on the processes and products of inquiry.

RESOURCES FOR INQUIRY

The widespread undersupport of teacher education programs nationally, especially given the requirements of their clinical mission and the breadth of the intellectual underpinnings of teaching, is difficult for heads of teacher education to do much about on their own. Collectively, it may be possible to have some effect, especially now that the policy climate has at least warmed up.

Heavy instructional responsibilities, many of them clinical and field-based, make it difficult to set aside time for more directed efforts at inquiry. Expectations within the parent institutions that we engage in inquiry are not very high. Resources from foundations or the Federal government are very small, have diminished in recent years, and are not likely to increase in the immediate future. The widespread expectation that teacher educators can be freely called upon to donate their time because they get their psychic income from charity for the public good, while certainly explaining what has often happened in the past, is a poor foundation on which to rest the systematic advance of the profession. Careful comparative analysis of the relative allocations going to programs of comparable instructional type in each institution may prove helpful in the quest to enhance education faculty contribution to research and scholarship.

One under-attended-to resource for inquiry is that which we must apply for program evaluation purposes. It is required of all those of us who accept examination under national accreditation standards; many states are now expecting similar activities of programs they approve for certification purposes. Such inquiry can serve purposes beyond the purely local if it is conceptualized properly. It can also constitute an allocation of existing faculty time with which it will be difficult for senior academic officers to find disagreement.

The increased pressure on colleges and universities to relate more effectively to public education can also be turned to good advantage in terms of providing inquiry resources. Small amounts of additional effort can turn service projects into activities that can benefit others beyond the immediate service base by sharing what can be learned in such activities with others. That requires the application of inquiry frames to such activities and then expenditure of modest amounts of effort to share the results, approaches that can be more than justified in terms of the obligation of higher education not merely to give service but to do so in a context of both teaching and the advancement of knowledge.

PLANNING FOR POST-BACCALAUREATE PROGRAMS

Teacher education will become post-baccalaureate professional preparation. The program will probably be of two years duration closely combining clinical and didactic work. Field-based components of the program will need to be conducted in settings under the genuine joint control of the college and university and a cooperating school district. (Joint control means just that, neither partner just accommodating the needs and interests of the other but each insisting of the other what it needs to carry out its particular responsibilities in the partnership.)

Planning is difficult to undertake with so many uncertainties. Before the programs will fly, many other problems will need to be addressed and solved. Still, the conceptual work can begin. Important beginning points may be found in the work done on extended programs and in the design laid out in B. O. Smith's A Design for a School of Pedagogy.[1] Faculty may find that it takes more extensive familiarization to think in the ways implied by an insistence on grounding professional preparation programs on the knowledge base and the application of inquiry processes in practical settings. Developing a functional understanding of the different knowledge needs of practitioners (as contrasted to academics), especially as teachers think and act holistically in treating the creative requirements of the design tasks continually facing them, will entail considerable thought and deliberation, the latter with solid representation from practitioner communities.

Not all teacher preparation colleges are in a position, of course, to think about a post-baccalaureate program because they are not authorized to offer masters or professional degrees. On the post-baccalaureate model, however, superior performance in the liberal arts and the academic major, and renewed attention to the adequacy of the fulfillment of such aims, should place baccalaureate-level institutions in a strong position as suppliers of the new teaching candidates.

FOUR PROBLEM AREAS

Four problem areas confront us. What are we to do with arguments traditionally made by many of our peers against standardizing approaches to teacher education? What should happen to teacher education programs unwilling to pursue their grounding on inquiry and its products? What should happen to teacher education programs whose professorial resources are inadequate to the task owing to the insufficient number of faculty to reflect fully the breadth of the knowledge base underpinning education? What is our role as heads of teacher education to foster such developments? These are difficult matters, but we must confront them.

Resistance across teacher education programs to the claim that there are certain things we must all do in common has always been substantial. At one level it has taken the form of the assertion by individual faculty members or teaching assistants that only they are individually in a position to decide what is to be taught in their sections. At another it is the claim that institutional diversity is healthy for education, both higher and lower, and efforts to standardize approaches to the training of teachers and administrators should be opposed.

Both arguments have a certain validity. But they also conceal important truths. If the teacher education curriculum is carefully drawn by an entire faculty (following, for example, a "white wall" exercise as described above), to what extent do individual teaching faculty have the right to alter the conception agreed upon? Not very much, is the only reasonable answer, unless one is willing to accept making a mockery of the effort expended in and the professional significance of the curriculum design task.

Similarly, the argument for diversity of teacher education programs makes a great deal of sense from the perspective of serving different views of the **purposes** of education. But that would be analogous to allowing diversity in the training of physicians on grounds that the purposes of health may be varyingly interpreted, too. That is not to say that there will not in any professional field be "schools" of thought that will capture adherents, wax and wane, and enliven the debates among its members. But the core will be well defined, and all participants will certainly expect common acquisition of some minimum number of conceptual and practical skills. In respect to that core, diversity is served only at the expense of professionals being able to work effectively together; if they cannot depend upon a commonality of background, cooperation and coordination become exceedingly difficult.

Teacher education programs which do not actively pursue their connection to the processes and products of inquiry are another matter. In the short run, we can afford to be tolerant and developmentally supportive. Over the long haul, however, inadequate connection to the knowledge bases and the techniques by which they are advanced should become reason for denial of the further participation in the privilege of preparing teachers.

The third area of potential controversy has to do with the critical mass issue. Surely for teacher preparation, as for medicine, engineering, or law, there must be some lower limit of staffing below which it is not possible to provide the intellectual resources or the professional expertise requisite to train teachers. Number of faculty is not everything, of course; what they **do** is critically important, too. But at some lower level, be it five, seven, twelve, or twenty-five faculty, teacher education programs can only barely provide their students with sufficient expertise for professional instructional purposes.

Part of the task for teacher education is coming to terms with this crucial resource question. Defining the knowledge base for teacher education will establish the parameters for required faculty expertise. Once that step is taken, then it will be necessary for the teacher education arm of the profession and individual institutional leaders to act on its implications. Far too many inadequately staffed and ineffectively operated teacher education programs exist. Such programs must be strengthened and corrected or be terminated.[2]

The fourth problem area has to do with the internal politics of teacher education. Real centripetal forces seem to be at work in our arena which hamper our ability to turn to the important tasks. We are a diverse lot of institutions. We find it difficult to agree among ourselves about where we should be going and how. Rhetorically we agree on many things, but practical steps involve actions which threaten our cohesiveness if not, for some of us, apparently, our very livelihood. Courage and compassion will be required, but the ultimate frame of reference must be the broader purposes we serve, not narrow self interest. The months and years immediately ahead of us will be trying. A dispassionate forecast would have to suggest a shakeout period over the next decade in teacher education that will yield quite different programs and institutional configurations for carrying out the professional preparation responsibilities. Its effects on the organizations and voluntary agencies to which some (but by no means all) of us subscribe will not be without drama. Whether tragedy, mystery, farce, or heroic saga is in no small measure still in our own hands.

MEMO FIVE

To: Director, National Institute of Education (NIE)

As the chief administrator of the nation's lead agency for educational research, your capacity to aid in the reconceptualization of the education profession is very substantial. Principal areas in which NIE can be of increasingly greater assistance include the following.

DESIGN STUDIES FOR THE STRUCTURE OF INQUIRY-BASED SCHOOLS

Design studies should be launched aimed at developing alternative models of entire schools structured to rest on the knowledge bases of education, engage in practice-directed inquiry, and be more continuously responsive to developments in other parts of the practice and research and development communities. Initial efforts ought not to seek definitive outcomes, but be broadly exploratory aimed at raising sights and provoking discussion and commentary from the academic and practitioner commnunities alike. As the concepts mature, more deliberate attempts to define actual roles and responsibilities, support structures, and training models can then be undertaken.[1]

CAPTURING THE TECHNOLOGY OF EDUCATIONAL DEVELOPMENT

One of the needs NIE ought to meet is capturing, organizing, and otherwise rendering more conscious and explicit the technology of educational development. Awareness of the fugitive nature of much of the written material pertaining to such matters emerged as I sought citations to lead interested readers to materials descriptive of some of the processes to which the educational policy community ought to give greater attention. I did find some to support the material in Chapter Five, but when I found how little there was I realized that those of us who served as research administrators during the sixties and seventies were privy to a dialogue and an information flow (in the form of conversations, site visits, and the monitoring of project proposals and progress reports) that has not yet been adequately documented or captured for wider consumption. A modest project should be mounted to meet this goal. The review of the proposals, progress reports, and final reports of the major curriculum development activities of the National Science Foundation, U.S. Office of Education, Office of Economic Opportunity, and NIE, interviews with former project directors and participants, and consultation with industry and Defense Department officials where the technology of materials development continues would provide the raw material on the basis of which helpful handbooks for educational development can be prepared.

REVISION OF CURRICULUM DEVELOPMENT POLICY

Some years ago NIE adopted a sharply delimited curriculum development policy. Effective teaching materials, however, are one of the cornerstones of sound instruction. Such materials must be carefully developed, tested, and then made available with support materials to assure proper use by instructional staff. The current NIE policy permits only the development of prototype materials; the completion of final versions together with the necessary professional development materials designed to assure their effective use is now proscribed. In short, NIE's policy effectively prevents the completion of one of the crucial steps in assuring utilization of research results in instructional practice.

Two reasons for this policy limitation do exist. One is the relative cost of curriculum development. Fully developed, a single year-long course of instruction can cost $6 million or more. This is a small amount of money amortized over millions of potential students, but relative to the very small appropriations available, such costs are prohibitive. The second reason is the extreme sensitivity that has arisen because of two kinds of political considerations. The first of these is concern over the the proper Federal role in education. The second had to do with politicized objections over the specific content of one major curriculum development project, Man: A Course of Study (MACOS); great exception was taken by a narrow but politically insistent special interest group.[2]

The concern over the proper Federal role is a legitimate one, if curriculum development were undertaken to limit or control the choices available to teachers and local schools. On the other hand, if the Federal role aimed at the creation of responsible alternatives that would not exist absent Federal involvement, that would be quite another matter. A prospective Federal role in curriculum development oriented to the creation of viable alternatives also suggests the strategy to overcome narrow objections to curricular aims and content. NIE needs to reconsider and reformulate its curriculum development policy in anticipation of greater resources to bring the fruits of research and development on learning and curriculum to American schools and colleges.

KNOWLEDGE REVIEWS

Some work of this kind is now done, principally under the auspices of ERIC (Educational Resources Information Center), but much more needs to be undertaken. One of the most important needs is to provide materials to practitioner-based organizations for distribution to their members as well as to all teacher training institutions for use in on-going processes of curricular redesign. Knowledge reviews need to be written with specific audiences in mind; they are not profitably undertaken in the abstract. At the present time knowledge reviews, while useful, have tended to be done only on an occasional basis, even where the "occasions" have been specifically requested by one or another official at NIE. The preparation of knowledge reviews, targeted to varieties of professional audiences, needs to be regularized. Keying to different audiences is not enough; the documents need to be coordinated with one another. (For example, curriculum work will have bearing on the training of teachers, administrators, and supervisors as well as for those already performing those roles. Each is a separate audience with quite different reference groups, professional networks, and incentive systems, yet all clearly bear definable relations to the common concern of curricular innovation.) Reaching all the different audiences in coordinated fashion will take careful planning for dissemination as well as advance consideration of how to render the subject material meaningful given the range of studies, the different approaches taken, and the gaps that necessarily exist in the research because of the relatively small amounts of work yet done.

R&D SYSTEM STUDIES

The legislation establishing the National Institute of Education charges it with attending to the health and development of the research and development system in support of education. While NIE has made occasional efforts in that direction, no sustained effort has been mounted.[3] Candidly, it is not the kind of work that will bring either educators or legislators jumping out of their respective chairs. Still, much more study in this area can be done and must be. Some of the data can be generated and analyzed as part and parcel of the administration of the NIE grant and contract effort. Work elsewhere in the Federal government can be studied through inter-agency coordination mechanisms that now exist. Effective use might be made of non-governmental research administration interest groups that exist within professional organizations interested in educational research or across State and local (particularly large urban) school districts.

Some of the necessary work, however, is conceptual. This essay, for example, espouses a view of the R&D system for education which is very broad, much broader than large numbers of people familiar with research and development activities in other sectors, would be willing to accept. Of such disagreements are vigorous and important policy discussions constituted. A service sector endeavoring to use behavioral and social inquiry as a mechanism for systematizing service improvement cannot simply adopt language or concepts more appropriate to other research and development sectors; research administrators must attend to the distinctive requirements of the sector in which they work, and conceive of the appropriate policy and program initiatives accordingly. Others, no doubt, would argue with that proposition. At least there would be a discussion flowing, out of which purposive behavior could evolve. At present, there is next to no discussion, and what there is finds itself hastily appended or quickly stimulated (as, indeed, in part this essay itself was by the now-ongoing lab/center competition) only to subside in the face of the press of close-at-hand decision-making.

WHAT SUBSTANTIVE DECISIONS SHOULD NIE BE MAKING?

This topic could be considered as part of the R&D system studies but it is important enough to be singled out for special treatment. Educational policy in America is Federal, not national. Certain important matters, however, would not be given attention unless the national interest were clearly asserted and served. If this is not done, then desirable options for States and localities (as previously argued in the section on curriculum policy, for example) might not otherwise be made available. A crucial issue, however, is what substantive decisions about educational research and developmnent ought to be made either by the NIE or under its auspices. (The distinction refers, for example, to the difference between NIE officials themselves making decisions and their setting up mechanisms whereby panels of persons representing academic disciplines or definable interests within the system make recommendations with the effective force of decisions).

Defining the proper parameters for NIE decision-making is not a simple matter. More is involved than confronting the reality of diverse political jurisdictions. Basic differences of view in how inquiry of different kinds can support educational practice must be confronted. The fact of different epistemological perspectives **vis a vis** "reality" raises profound doubts about the legitimacy of some academic elitist views of the proper pyramids of expertise which ought to be permitted to make decisions and do the work. (That statement is **NOT** an apology for supporting incompetent work; it most definitely **IS** an observation that hegemonic behavior within the research and broader academic community has far too often worked effectively to claim predominance or exclusivity where greater pluralism should have prevailed.)

Effective examples of advisers representing very different constituencies of educational research -- researchers, policy makers, teachers, teacher educators, laypersons, academics -- committed to work intensively with one another do exist. Such mixed groups in the past have been able to reach productive mutual understandings that furthered the work of education and the health and productivity of the research and development community.

How NIE understands its decision-making reach in educational research depends heavily on its views about what educational research is, what systems it serves, how it serves those systems, and who other potential actors are. If complete clarity cannot be achieved (because that may be too much to ask for), then at least care and effort needs to be expended on these points.

INSTITUTIONAL SUPPORT FOR INQUIRY IN TEACHER EDUCATION

No better illustration of the thinness of the thinking about the R&D system in support of education can be seen than in the failure to realize that the most important dissemination mechanism in place is the teacher training enterprise in America. The relatively low involvement of the overwhelming majority of teacher training institutions in the development and operation of programs of teacher preparation functioning, in effect, as knowledge dissemination instruments, if allowed to continue, virtually guarantees maintenance of a non-inquiry-based training model. Failure to see teacher training institutions as the critical initial dissemination element only compounds the problem.

The non-involvement of teacher training institutions was not accidental. The thinly veiled contempt within the educational research agencies of the past for teacher educators and the programs they operate has only begun to subside; many would argue that if the tide has changed, it is hardly flowing full bore yet. The almost deliberate manner in which the Federal policy apparatus worked to minimize involvement of teacher education programs in the developing inquiry efforts of the late 1960's is all the more astonishing in retrospect, because such exclusion became something of a self-fulfilling prophecy. Even those strong, primarily graduate institutions with a very substantial and exciting research enterprise for education have had uncertain results in connecting, organizationally and curricularly, what they have been doing for inquiry with what they have been doing for professional preparation, so different have the two groups of academics been in their orientations.

To remedy non-involvement in and/or disconnection between inquiry and training over the long haul I urge you to begin planning for a major (by present standards) institutional support program to encourage inquiry and the application of its products in the principal teacher education institutions of the Nation. Grants would be made on a three-year renewable basis to teacher education programs of a certain faculty size (aiming at the major teacher producers) to any institution that was prepared to use the money to support inquiry and related activities bearing on education (the money could not be used to hire fulltime faculty). The funds could be used as seed money for inquiry, for the partial release of faculty for research, for curriculum redesign incorporating new research findings, for inservice work with teachers to share the results of inquiry, for consultant services to schools for similar purposes, for the purchase of necessary inquiry equipment, and the like. Grants would be renewable on presentation of evidence that the preceding grant period had been devoted to expenditures in the approved class. An average grant of $50,000, providing such support to 400 institutions would cost $20,000,000, a small investment, really, to orient the profession as a whole to the outcomes and processes of inquiry. A parallel small grant program of $1 million for grants of $10,000 or less could be set aside at the same time to support those vitally interested in inquiry in the smaller teacher education programs for inquiry and related purposes specified in the grant request. Such a program probably ought not be considered a permanent addition to NIE's appropriation request because, on the conceptualization advanced here for a major change in the basic assumptions underpinning professional function, small teacher education programs are almost certain to be phased out in time.

This proposal is certain to raise a certain amount of protest from those institutions whose size would deny them access to these vital inquiry resources. What is more, such institutions outnumber the larger producers by approximately two to one. Realities are realities, however. The smaller number of bigger institutions is where the overwhelming number of teaching candidates are graduated. It is they who must be strengthened in regard to the knowledge base and its application and only they who have a reasonable chance of fully being able to gain such strength. Of course, it is not just numbers or size alone, but the fact that the extensive range of expertise required to participate in intellectually sound preparation programs cannot be provided by a small handful of faculty.[4]

MAINTAINING AND EXPANDING THE SYSTEM OF LABS AND CENTERS

The desirability of supporting strong, independent regional educational laboratories and university-based research and development centers is strongly implied by the characteristics of behavioral and social inquiry presented in Part Two.

Regional educational laboratories were first created in the mid sixties to support educational development and linkage functions between R&D and the schools. The organizations are governed by boards broadly representative of the practitioner and policy communities in a region. They tie, therefore, to the many stakeholders in educational research and development and are responsible for important bridging functions between theoretical knowledge and the improvement of practice. Because of their regional orientation, the organizational commitment to them engendered by their governance structure, and the promise of their work, the regional laboratories have been a strong force for stability in the rough political and economic environments of the last half dozen years (a point that ought not be lost on the research policy community). Nonetheless, some have seen that political reality as a problem to be overcome rather than a strength to capitalize upon. The differences of view have a great deal to do with operating conceptions of the nature of the R&D enterprise and also who should be making what kinds of decisions about educational research and development.

The character of behavioral and social inquiry in support of education, especially a Federally-organized system, strongly suggests the viability and validity of the regional laboratory initiative. Support for the institutions should be substantially increased; the presently contemplated expansion from seven to ten should be followed in the years ahead by a doubling to, perhaps, twenty, as rapidly as the trained personnel can be provided. One technique for accomplishing this might be to consider splitting the institutions two for one as their current size increases. NIE's role in respect to laboratories should be supportive, coordinative, and developmental, managing the grants awarded to create and maintain institutional strength regionally.

The importance of the university-based research and development centers also arises from the character of social and behavioral inquiry for education. Scale of effort is important. So is continuity. Collaborative planning from multiple perspectives, especially as applied to the R&D centers' central themes, has proven extremely effective in raising standards in educational research and improving its focus. The real progress in educational research generally since the R&D Center program was launched under the old Cooperative Research authority has been no accident. The lessons learned from the support of the program over the years suggests the desirability of increasing the number of centers (but not their size) as resources and organized institutional capacities in educational research present themselves.[5]

HIGHER EDUCATION RESEARCH

The widespread unwillingness of higher education institutions to launch studies of themselves or to conduct institutional research other than that concerned with the important but excessively narrowly conceived production functions of higher education, reflects a negative climate for the examination of higher education functions and responsibilities. That has a consequential effect on higher education's close relationship with lower education. The institution responsible for training education professionals is not, in respect to what it does, an inquiring setting. It is not too surprising that schools themselves do not see themselves that way, either.

Scholars love to study everybody but themselves. For every hundred studies on infants and elementary school children there are ten on adolescents and secondary school students but barely one on higher education and its processes. (If those numbers are not exactly right, the order of magnitude is.) Increasing the responsiveness of the larger education system to the processes and products of inquiry means stimulating and supporting far more attention to higher education research than heretofore. The orientation to inquiry must begin there, too. NIE, therefore, needs to increase substantially its investments in research and development for higher education.

LONG RANGE PLANNING

Finally, NIE needs to undertake much more comprehensive and systematic long range planning. The context for that planning is not the identification of specific projects that need doing; in fact, the less of that NIE does, the better it is likely to be for research and for the education community. As suggested earlier, when NIE makes decisions it ought to be operating more in a "ratification" mode of the recommendations of others. NIE's long-range planning, therefore, should focus on how to maintain and enhance the R&D capabilities for the educational system of the nation as a whole and what it means to do so.

NIE's planning should be casting alternative images of what the R&D support system for education ought to look like in ten, twenty, and thirty years and considering what the implications of that might be for the organization of the educational system and the training and retraining of its personnel. The images thus generated will work backwards on policymakers and the education community to guide and support the decisions formulated in the short-term. Such planning should not be thought of as the "preparation of detailed drawings" but rather the developing of guiding images for the entire profession.

For several years now, NIE has been struggling with steadily declining appropriations. The struggles to prevent three, seven, or nineteen million dollar reductions in NIE's budget have been frustrating, but they have also necessarily restricted the vision of all the policy actors away from what ought to be in the longer run. Change the frame of reference. Simply assume that the educational systems of the Nation require far more substantial support through the various instrumentalities of educational research and development. What **would** an NIE budget in excess of $1 billion to usher in the 21st century look like?

$300 million - Regional Educational Laboratories

An appropriation of this size would permit 15-20 laboratories to have budgets commensurate with their research linkage responsibilities and to engage in curriculum and other kinds of development projects associated with regionally-situated educational needs.

$50 million - Research and Development Centers

Wherever there are sufficiently large aggregations of research talent and interest to justify their support, NIE should sponsor Research and Development Centers for education. Ranging in size from $.5 million to $2 million a year, these centers should orient themselves more to emerging leads arising from their work than to narrowly prescribed missions which can be better served through commissioned policy research or discrete development projects. This budget line would support approximately fifty such centers housed primarily in universities but also in other research organizations.

$150 million - Unsolicited Project Research

Using traditional panel decision processes, NIE should support unsolicited project research at this level. Panels should include researchers with a liberal sprinkling of other stakeholder representatives. Funds should be administered in a fashion that guarantees a third is available for new starts in any given year.

$75 million - Policy Research

Such work should include the National Assessment of Educational Progress, the National Center for Educational Statistics, major evaluation studies, and other policy-oriented studies including work in education futures. Work should be launched only after careful consultation with Congressional figures, representative State authorities, the Education Commission of the States, practitioner and stakeholder organizations, and the like.

$300 million - Curriculum Materials and Instructional Equipment Development

One of the most powerful ways in which to assure instructional practice rests on knowledge is to embed such knowledge in materials and equipment. Furthermore, regular attention to materials development in all the many areas of curricular concern is a way of guaranteeing currency. $300 million a year would assure the support of fifty new major curriculum or other development projects on a six year cycle. It would permit the systematic pursuit of curricular alternatives to preserve local and State options. It would also presume the operation of an effective advisory and sensing mechanism designed to assure that the development projects launched would meet major needs identified throughout the country.

$50 million - Institutional Support for Schools, Colleges, and Departments of Education

This amount continues in expanded form in the NIE budget because of the belief that over nearly twenty years of experiences with institutional support of this kind its worth will have been proven, but not sufficiently to overcome the heavy pressures at the State and institutional level to use local resources to support direct instructional responsibilities and the demands for service.

$50 million - Dissemination

This line would support the ERIC centers, plus the conduct of knowledge reviews and development of targeted communications to discrete practitioner and stakeholder audiences.

$150 million and expanding - Practitioner Institutes

Even though by this time newly structured schools would allow substantially increased amounts of time for ongoing professional development and continuing education integral to the school day, a burgeoning R&D enterprise will be generating all kinds of knowledge-based innovations about which practitioners must learn. An ongoing and expanding institute program would support the orderly transmission of knowledge and expertise in the utilization of new materials and techniques. Living costs and stipends would be provided to teachers and other practitioners to participate periodically in such activities. Institutes might be conducted during summer months or on an academic year basis.

Total - $1.125 billion

For tomorrow a budget such as this would be irresponsible. For the turn of the century it is a reasonable goal, indeed, essential to steady improvement of instruction and more effective service by the Nation's schools and colleges.

MEMO SIX

To: Executive Director
National Council for the Accreditation of Teachers Education (NCATE)

The place of national accreditation of teacher education programs in a Federal system where certification occurs at the State level has been and will continue to be a warmly debated issue. The tremendous diversity of institutional size and character and its consequences for teacher education have long troubled teacher education and will certainly not disappear quickly. What constitutes leadership for teacher education nationally and how can it be asserted? This memo does not pretend to cover all aspects of these three issues. It does suggest steps that might be taken to further the process now under way to implement the new standards structure recently approved by the NCATE Board, standards which highlight the importance of inquiry and the knowledge base underpinning teacher education.

Those institutions presenting themselves for national accreditation ought to be those who are also willing to demonstrate their commitment to inquiry and acting on the knowledge base. Such a commitment can be demonstrated in a variety of ways. Those who are engaged in formal research and development will have products to show, and certainly any institution offering advanced preparation programs (that is, beyond initial certification) will want to be able to demonstrate that its faculty are, in effect, performing as research "masters" to which their students can be considered "apprenticed."

Not all institutions need or ought to offer advanced preparation programs; if they do not, perhaps they ought not to be obliged to be active performers of formal inquiry. They must, however, still be able to display their connection to inquiry done elsewhere by the content of their curriculum, for example. They should also be able to show their own commitment to engaging in the kinds of practice-based inquiry appropriate for the teacher education function per se.

EVIDENCE CATEGORIES[1]

NCATE's task, then, is to consider guidelines for assessing the inquiry climate of institutions presenting themselves for accreditation. The evidence categories presented below are illustrative. Not all of them need to be met by every institution, but clearly some of them do, e.g., evidence of formal program evaluation studies.

Faculty Publications

Direct evidence of faculty research and scholarly productivity can be found in publication records. In addition, to the extent that publications are in refereed journals or volumes, they constitute evidence of positive peer evaluation.

Program Evaluation Studies

Program evaluations can take numerous forms ranging all the way from quite formal assessments to simple requests for letters of feedback from graduates and their employers. Evidence that program evaluation is conducted by teacher education institutions commensurate with the size, complexity, and diversity of programs says a great deal about inquiry climate. Even more compelling would be evidence that the evaluation study results are actually used in making program modifications.

Inquiry Activity Record

Apart from formal products resulting from inquiry, institutions may also be able to document the existence of on-going inquiry activities.

Internal Research Organization

Some institutions may be able to describe the manner in which they are organized to stimulate and support the conduct of or attention to inquiry. The existence of faculty research "clusters," budget lines in support of research, assigned responsibilities for research and related activity, and so on would be helpful indicators.

Grants

Evidence of grant-seeking, successful or not, documents efforts to support research and scholarship and provides a basis for evaluating its sophistication and/or connectedness to the prime professional missions of the institution.

Pursuit of Collaborative Models

Institutions may be able to show that their inquiry activities are undertaken collaboratively, that is, across disciplines and professional domains, or cooperatively with practitioners. Where they can they are displaying their awareness of the importance of multiple perspectives in carry out behavioral and social inquiry.[2]

Library and Analysis Resources

Current journal collections, acquisition records, and use patterns can help establish the vitality of the scholarly effort. Similarly, the availability of data tapes and facilities to undertake secondary analysis (and maybe even consultant help in the process) are increasingly important indicators of capability and commitment to inquiry.

Instructional Load

An absolutely fundamental indicator of inquiry climate is instructional load. There are many ways of calculating it, and the data need to be examined quarter by quarter or semester by semester to understand completely what the data describe. To relate to inquiry, either by engaging in it or monitoring and reflecting on the work of others, faculty members cannot spend all of their time in instructional duties. There must be time for continuous professional development, for writing, and for independent or collaborative scholarship or research. If it cannot be found in the records pertaining to faculty effort, it is unlikely that it is taking place.

Knowledge-Grounded Professional Preparation Programs

Whether teacher education programs go through the more elaborate "white wall" exercise described in the memo to heads of teacher education or something less formal, they ought to be able to document the manner in which they warrant the content and process of their curricula on the basis of current knowledge. The evidence may be in the form of curriculum planning papers or syllabi. Whatever its form, it should be capable of being compared to current knowledge syntheses periodically made available to accreditation site visitors.

A QUESTION OF STANCE

An old question has challenged NCATE now and again. That is whether the accreditation standards should be understood as developmental in character, an incentive to raise up levels of performance, or whether they should be seen as templates against which to measure institutions. Those that measure up are in; those that do not are out.

The place where proponents of both positions stand depends in some measure on how strong they think their own institutions are and what they think the field as a whole needs or can stand. The issue is complicated, as we all know, by the fact that national accreditation in teacher education is purely voluntary, and no State, which is where the power to issue certificates lies, has to care at all about NCATE's judgments. States can decide to approve any institutions for teacher preparation they care to, and many do just that. Some even approve institutions for teacher certification which cannot pass the major institutional regional accreditation reviews.

In such a climate and circumstance, how heightened standards pertaining to inquiry are to be applied by the visiting teams and the Council itself, is something to consider carefully. Serious thought should be given to a two-stage cycle of, say, seven to eight years for each stage. During the first stage the standards could be applied developmentally, but in the second stage failure to meet them would be grounds for non-accreditation.

MEMO SEVEN

To: Members of the Research and Development Community

This memo is directed to you in your dual capacity as performers of research and development and as trainers of the next generations of performers. If the characteristics of behavioral and social inquiry have been accurately presented in this paper, then there are more than a few implications for your two roles.

REFLECTING MULTIPLE PERSPECTIVES

The metaphorical dimension in behavioral and social inquiry plus the unavoidability of the presence of values in its pursuit require that researchers be sensitive to the existence and implications of multiple perspectives.[1] As a minimum, researchers must be broadly literate in the behavioral and social sciences and in the arts and humanities. They must be conversant with fundamental epistemological differences reflected in the perspectives of academics, practitioners, and those who expect to be served by schools and universities. The methodological richness of educational inquiry must be fully explored in research training, not only because of the variety of tools which it represents, but because of what it can teach about diverse perspectives. Awareness that inquiry can compare outcomes of educational treatments, experimentally test theoretical concepts, analyze educational settings ethnographically, review archival material historically, analyze detailed behavior in small numbers of cases, undertake conceptual analyses, review demographic data, meta-analyze empirical findings on a specific research topic, or attempt to construct and validate new techniques for education based on existing research foundations (to name just a few) should help researchers better place the work they propose to undertake within larger frames of reference.

When members of the research community increase their level of sensitivity to the presence and validity of the several perspectives forthcoming not only from different branches of formal inquiry but also from practitioners, policy makers, and the clients of schools, one important fringe benefit should be a reduction in researchers' propensity to engage in behavior which others might characterize as "shooting oneself in the foot." Criticism is absolutely essential to the progress of formal inquiry; most scholars enjoy a good scrap over methodological and conceptual issues in their field. As long as such bouts are confined to the narrow boundaries of academe, little harm is done. The trouble with behavioral and social inquiry, however, whether researchers like it or not, is that what they say is very often immediately interpretable or understandable by those responsible for practice and policy. This places special burdens on those in the research community to prepare their critiques mindful not only of their academic targets but also of the potential effects in other sectors.[2] Researchers are no more immune from verbal overkill than anyone else. Avoiding the Scylla of too-gentle critique only to sail inextricably into the Charybdis of jeopardizing the entire research approach by conveying impressions that nothing is known or that all the efforts of research are "sound and fury" is a burden that falls on the research community. Knowledge of the impact and worth of multiple perspectives and different epistemologies should prove helpful charting aids.

VALUES

Closely related to the importance of multiple perspectives is the value embeddedness of inquiry in support of education. Explicit attention to this, in the design, conduct, and reporting of inquiry, is mandatory for the research community. If we could depend upon attention to valuational considerations in the undergraduate curriculum, we might not have to worry quite as much, but few liberal education programs approach this directly nor do most teacher education programs from which significant numbers of education graduate students come. Recognizing values in the disciplines, methodologies, and conceptual frames of reference of research is not always easy. There are approaches to examining for values, including exposing proposed work to value critique before it is undertaken, or utilizing the mechanism of collaboration with pertinent stakeholders, such as representatives of different cultural groups or practitioners, in designing and conducting research.

To recognize that values are embedded in educational inquiry is also to point to the importance of generating multi-cultural awareness in the research community. Vigorous and effective efforts in affirmative action in the recruitment of graduate students for research training and in the employment of research and related personnel are also logical derivatives of this understanding even if we were not under pre-existing and wholly valid obligations on other grounds.

A third approach to systematic incorporation of awareness of the values dimension in educational inquiry is to develop a capacity and habit, in research training and in the design of research, for stakeholder analysis. Stakeholders are those who stand to gain or lose as a consequence of a piece of inquiry. It is not necessary for a stakeholder to know about a piece of work being done in order to have a stake in it. The human subjects of a research project, for example, have a very direct stake in what is happening, and procedures are well established for coping with the real interests present here. Once one goes beyond the immediate participants in a piece of research, however, the issues are even more difficult to fathom, but that is not a justification for ignoring the attempt to do so. Researchers ought to feel obligated to consider who the stakeholders are in respect to a given piece of inquiry might be, what their stakes are, and whether sufficient attention to the interests thus revealed has been given. Attending to stakeholder interests, of course, does not necessarily mean accommodating them. At the very least consideration ought to be given to such matters; when it is, insights about alternative perspectives almost always emerge.

ACHIEVING CLARITY ON INQUIRY'S RELATION TO PRACTICE

Researchers need to clarify their conceptions of how inquiry relates to the improvement of practice, how such conceptions inform their own work, and how to assist research trainees in so framing their forthcoming work. As suggested in Chapter Seven, there are many models of that relationship, all useful for their specific purposes, each reflective of its basic assumptions and the purposes of its proponents. If researchers gave more explicit attention to the relationship of their work to the worlds of practice it would help them better keep in mind the specific directions of their collaborative responsibilities, as well as suggest how the results of their work ought to be disseminated, and to whom. To help them in this regard, researchers, present and future, might wish to undertake the obligation to consider, **before** as well as **after** the conduct of their inquiry, the probability, desirablility, feasibility, and consequences of the application of their work, an examination that begins first with consideration of what would **constitute** application and by **whom.** This proposition clearly includes the prospect that a given piece of inquiry is neither intended nor ready for application. Researchers' obligations under such circumstances, to both practitioners and the rest of the research community, can be met by suitable disclaimers and cautions, as well as appropriately limited dissemination strategies.

WORKING TO OVERCOME UNWARRANTED STATUS HIERARCHIES

Great initial responsibility for the tensions that sometimes exist between the academy and practitioners rests with the academy. Some of this tension is wholly accidental, a consequence of academics' primary orientation to their peers and to the specialized languages they develop to communicate within the academic community. Scholars are expected to help others, however, but they often come across as off-putting. Asking scholars to "watch their language," however, is not enough; neither is it reasonable or helpful counsel to recommend homogenization of capacity or conceptualization.

It would be helpful, though, if the research commnunity developed greater sensitivity to others' perceptions of researchers' own sense of self-importance. Unwarranted status hierarchies get in the way of the communications that need to take place. They inject extraneous obstacles in an already difficult situation. While not all of the responsibility rests with scholars (some of the tension no doubt arises from projected insecurities from practitioners), the work of the research community finds its ultimate justification in the improvements in practice and the achievements of learners, not in the more limited rewards and recognitions of the research community. Incorporation of the concepts of stakeholders, multiple perspectives, values, different epistemologies, and the prospects of application should go a long way toward "inoculating" scholars against "status fever." Anything else researchers can do to work toward the unification of the larger profession of education embracing scholars and practitioners would be worthwhile.

MEMO EIGHT

To: Executive Directors, Practitioner-Based Organizations

Please consider the memo directed to teachers and principals and to follow up on the implications of what is said there within the context of your associational responsibilities. I also suggest the following courses of action.

INFORMING THE RESEARCH COMMUNITY

One of the most important contributions you can make is to develop and present to appropriate organizations and agencies well-ordered research agendas or, at least, topics on which help is needed. The American Educational Research Association, the National Institute of Education, and the Regional Educational Laboratories are three of these kinds of organizations. Others might include the National Institutes of Health, the National Science Foundation, the National Endowments for the Arts and for the Humanities, and discipline-based associations in the behavioral and social sciences.

Developing agendas of this kind requires continuous effort and periodic reassessment based on examination of inquiry undertaken over time. It may be more fruitful to seek to launch such efforts on a collaborative basis with appropriate units of major research-oriented associations or government agencies. The development and maintenance of agendas of the sort called for is difficult to undertake on an occasional basis; some ongoing mechanism within your associations may need to be created, with continuity achieved through such a device as staggering the membership terms of the individuals on the committee or group responsible for constructing the research agendas.

ORGANIZE OWN STUDY EFFORTS

Using the resources of ERIC and through continuous monitoring of the journal literature, organizations such as yours can mine the research literature from the particular perspectives of your membership. A certain amount of this effort has always gone on. This suggestion is principally a call to increase substantially its amount and intensity. It is not inconceivable that such work might come to be supported under dissemination grants from the National Institute of Education or other units within the Department of Education.

DEFINING PRACTICE-BASED INQUIRY ROLES AND ACTIVITIES

This essay has argued for a conception of the profession of education as engaged in inquiry throughout, not simply in the higher education community. Practitioner-based organizations could make important contributions toward this objective by stimulating consideration of the requirements for inquiry in the responsibilities of practitioners as their roles are currently defined. What in teacher, principal, counselor, or school psychologist daily activity might be classed as inquiry? What are its unique requirements and characteristics (for example, its holistic character and its orientation not to knowing but to doing)? Examining these questions would help accomplish both short-term and long-term objectives of this approach to render professional service more effective.

The short-term objective would be better to equip newly trained practitioners for their currently defined roles. The long-term objective is to begin to re-examine the structure of schools better to aid in the conduct of the kinds of inquiry required continuously to improve professional effectiveness on site.

Defining practice-based inquiry roles is different from the agenda-setting function suggested first. Here the focus is on the processes of a given professional role examined in an inquiry frame. The objective would be to highlight what kinds of inquiry and design strategies need to be learned to be able to perform the roles, and to determine what is required to facilitate the on-site, in-professional-role learning that enables those strategies to succeed.

One of the important outcomes of this kind of analysis is likely to be the documentation of the need for greater professional autonomy in the performance of practitioner roles than is now willingly granted by administrative superiors or lay authorities. The issue of autonomy -- what it means, why it is necessary, where its limits lie -- will be raised with increasing justification as the power of practice increases proportionally with its dependence on the knowledge base and inquiry strategies. The requirements of better and more timely data on which to ground immediate instructional decisions and the prospect of such data emerging from practitioner-based inquiry underscore the importance of autonomy to adopt that inquiry mode and act on its fruits when the need arises.

MEMO NINE

To: Representatives of Stakeholder Organizations

In the memorandum to researchers a stakeholder was defined as anyone who stood to gain or lose something as a result of research. This memorandum is directed to the representatives of stakeholder organizations, organized groups who seek to be served -- or better served -- by our educational institutions. Included would be PTA's, Councils for Exceptional Children, groups representative of various minority populations, organizations for the gifted, the Council for Basic Education, and so on. The net is intentionally large here and the mesh small.

A primary impetus for reform in the directions called for will come through the continuous pressure for more effective service by schools and universities and the willingness to call for and support the provision of justifiable resources for doing so. **Incessant demand for accountability in performance is a necessary prerequisite to the professional advance called for here.** Also, your general support of the proposition that the education profession ought to act on the basis of knowledge and systematic inquiry would be welcome on its face.

A few somewhat more narrowly focused initiatives could also be taken.

STAKEHOLDER ANALYSIS

In particular, you should be especially insistent that stakeholder analysis comes to be applied regularly in research, research training, and in professional training, generally. Inquiry in support of education is never "innocent" in respect to values; the values reflected in inquiry are likely to have differential effects on stakeholder groups. Stakeholder analysis will increase the awareness of researchers and practitioners alike to this critical characteristic of behavioral and social inquiry in support of improved educational practice.

SUPPORTING INQUIRY REFLECTING MULTIPLE PERSPECTIVES

While it would be nice if the research and research policy communities would act on their own, it will not hurt if representatives of stakeholder groups press the importance of undertaking inquiry in the research and development sector from a variety of perspectives. Not only are there important policy and practical consequences of this posture, there are cost implications as well. Doing work on an issue or topic from several perspectives is going to be more expensive than doing it from one. Work from multiple perspectives is more nearly consistent with the nature of social reality, however, and, therefore, more likely to be of benefit to practitioners and those they are charged to serve.

A corollary of both emphases, multiple perspectives and stakeholder concern, is your insistence that the educational research community effectively accomplish its affirmative action goals. The availability of qualified investigators knowledgeable about and attuned to the needs and aspirations of various constituencies of schooling and capable of conducting the kind of inquiry and related activities of service to them must be assured.

VIGOROUS PRESENTATION OF STAKEHOLDER PERCEPTIONS OF REALITY

Three fundamental orientations resulting in differing epistemologies were identified in Chapter Seven, that of academics, that of practitioners, and that of the "clients" of schools. It is all too easy for academics or practitioners not to hear or apprehend the reality of those whom the schools would serve. To prevent error or distortion for such reasons, stakeholder communities and organizations can examine what the research community and the profession see as knowledge and also the processes both engage in to create knowledge. The press of one's responsibilities and the confirmatory evidence of one's professional peers can be overwhelming; the competing evidence from "outsiders to the fraternity" is difficult to hear, unless those presenting it are insistent and, perhaps, even noisy at times. Educational policy makers often think of their "constituencies" as the formal groups and associations with whom they work most closely. In a sense that is normal, even essential. But professionals are but means to the greater ends of the educational system. There have been and will be again many occasions where educators will need to be reminded of the ultimate purposes for which they work, and cautioned not to mistake the politics of their own working together as the prime forces to which they must attend. Forceful representations from stakeholder organizations can be very helpful in this regard.

MEMO TEN

To: Education Writers in the Popular Press and Your Editors

Education writers engage in inquiry, too. It is not the kind of inquiry that academics do but it is supposed to follow its own special rules and can be measured against criteria which are not all that dissimilar from those either researchers or practitioners have applied to them. In many respects, for good or ill, the inquiry conducted at your hands has been far more powerful in its influence on schools and the profession than any conducted by the research and development sector. All the more reason, then, to expect greater familiarity with the educational system, its complexity, and the diverse ways in which it can and must be understood.

INCREASING INQUIRY LITERACY AND RESISTING BIAS

Only a handful of those now working the education beat seem to have very much familiarity with behavioral and social science. Many of those who do seem rapidly to move on to other assignments, some of the best qualified, even, to the university setting. The predominant orientation, however, is that of a layperson, not bad, in itself, but not enough either. The public expects more -- and gets it -- on the financial pages. The public expects more -- and gets it -- from legal reporters or those covering medicine. Somehow, it has been permissable for the first assignment of new reporters to be education, good performance of which entitles them to advance to city hall, politics, or other more exciting duties.

In a sense, this practice has mimicked the values -- or opinions -- of the greater society. Of late, its judgments about the quality and status of education in national opinion polls, tax levy votes, and the letters columns have been made clear. The problem goes deeper, however.

TIME, for example, can editorialize on what it calls the "soft subject" of "Decision Making and Leadership Development" while a good portion of the parent public wishes that clear decisions and effective leadership everywhere characterize the schools their children attend; the bias in the reporter's language is clear.[1] As respected a political writer as Haynes Johnson can confuse the concepts of merit pay and master teachers[2] (but one has to be understanding here because even the Secretary of Education has admitted he had been doing the same for three months).[3]

A thoughtful letter by the principal of a parochial school to a Cincinnati paper elaborated on the view that the education debate needs to take greater note of "the social transformation of the country." The letter reviewed changes in the attitudes of parents, children, and teachers toward learning, teaching, and the schools and ended with the observation that perhaps, if we spent more time with our children, we wouldn't need to spend all that much money on schools. The bold headline accorded the letter was: "Money Can't Rectify School Shortcomings."[4] The blatant shift of focus from family circumstances to an outright assertion about schools is either malicious or incompetent. If it were an isolated instance it wouldn't be worth mentioning.

A somewhat more subtle but no less damaging example can be found in a recent Associated Press story on the release of a study completed by the National Center for Educational Statistics on behalf of The National Commission on Excellence in Education. The article cites the finding that only 5% of the sample of teacher education institutions surveyed had required teacher training beyond the traditional four-year program. The data were offered as evidence for the assertion that "education schools are resisting recommendations to require longer teacher training beyond the typical four years," a conclusion the writer apparently came to because the recommendation had been made repeatedly in testimony before the Commission.[5] To label the absence of something the product of resistance, however, had better be based on solid evidence. Consider the following analogy. Would we blame a clerk for resisting his physician when advised to eat red meat? The clerk doesn't follow his physician's advice because if he does, he won't have carfare to his job, and if he doesn't have carfare, he doesn't work, and if he doesn't work, he doesn't eat <u>anything</u> let alone red meat as his physician directed. A reporter who understood the territory would have recognized that forthright movement in the direction many teacher educators now recognize is essential to improvement **absent essential policy supports** would be tantamount to the commission of institutional suicide. The result would be the removal from the scene of precisely those teacher educators most needed.[6]

The objective in offering these examples is neither to antagonize nor unfairly castigate; it is to plead for more effective, less biased, more thoughtful, less simplistic presentation based on investigation (inquiry) that recognizes the realities of many variables, in complex relation, capable of being reasonably interpreted from a variety of perspectives. None of this awareness will be of much use, however, if facts, contexts, and explanations are distorted or unexplored.

RESISTING TEMPTATIONS TO OVERSIMPLIFY

A reporter's job is to reach the core of an issue or event and present it in a fashion that is understandable to her readers. There is always a dynamic tension between the fullness of the topic, the limitations of space, and the average capacities of the readership. It is not an easy job. The educational system, its aims, and its problems are not easily grasped, never wholly fathomable, nor necessarily agreed upon. Context is very important and difficult to present in the extreme limitations of space in the popular press.

But oversimplification should be strenuously avoided. It can happen very easily. For example, over the summer a great deal of press space[7] was devoted to a stimulating set of seminars for teachers supported by the National Endowment for the Humanities. The seminars permitted 225 secondary school teachers to refurbish the intellectual underpinnings of their disciplines by reading great books, discussing them with university faculty, going on museum outings, and attending theater productions.

Exciting? Yes. A general recipe for what ails American education? Only in the most limited sense. To provide **one** such exposure to the entire teaching staff in American schools at the level of investment of the summer experiment would have required more than $6 **billion** and **half** the fulltime resident instructional staff of the nation's four-year colleges. But none of the articles mentioned that unpleasant reality as they reported an exciting initiative only big money could create. The long-run effect of the summer's limited effort will, in all probability, itself be equally limited. Worse, it may well **increase** the sense of discontent because of the inability to meet the expectations improperly raised by journalistic attention absent either a sense of context or reportorial balance.

Controversy is easy to generate, difficult to channel, and almost always corrosive when it is unwarranted. The greatest oversimplifications in the popular press are those perpetrated by witty, credentialed, and well-placed figures whose work or whose comments are difficult for either editors or reporters (who after all live by language) to resist. America, it would seem, permits dilettantism in three sectors -- letters, politics, and education, but saying something well or provocatively does not make it true or justified. The popular press must develop sufficient expertise in the education domain to recognize when, by reporting the biases of an articulate few or giving space to people who either make up their data, never looked for it, or simply assume its existence, it may entertain the many but contribute little to the development of lasting solutions and steady improvement.

MEDIUMS AND MESSAGES

My comments to you are probably the most pointed in the entire set of recommendations I make in these memos. In some measure they may only reveal the extent of differences we may have over the proper responsibilities of the popular press. They certainly should not be read as arguing for favored treatment or less than critical analysis. Educators can -- and should -- be exposed to the most rigorous scrutiny of which you are capable.

Ultimately, the proper responsibility of the press may be to make money for its owners, and entertainment may be the best way of achieving that end. But the role of a press in a free society, where the citizenry votes on candidates, tax levies, and all manner of referenda, is to educate and inform. It is a common interest; in fact, the success of education and schooling is an enabling condition for the success of the newspapers and journals whose very survival is your livelihood. The popular press has about as many warts as educators; we would do well to help one another. Reporters who strive for excellence don't like being criticized any more than educators who do the same, each struggling within constraints over which neither has effective control.

The real cost of the weakness of education reporting and analysis in the popular press, however, is that its amateurism in respect to education contributes directly to the public perception that education is itself amateur. McLuhan's great truth that the medium is the message stands reaffirmed.

MEMO ELEVEN

To: College and University Presidents

The role of college and university presidents in helping to reconceptualize education in terms of the processes and products of inquiry is central. Your help is required in the following ways.

THE PLACE OF INQUIRY PROCESSES PERTAINING TO HIGHER EDUCATION

The application of inquiry to higher education's own processes has been exceedingly light. Foundation and government funds for such research have been minimal. As in lower education, other claims for internal resources have proven more persuasive or insistent. Even within individual departments relatively little investment is made on inquiry directed to the maintenance or enhancement of instructional quality. This has not been an institutional priority, by and large; indeed, when it has been addressed at all it has been defined as the responsibility of the individual faculty member.

Given that higher education is where all manner of certificated school personnel are initially trained, it is not surprising that what is true for higher education is mirrored in lower. A place to start, then, is to consider why higher education itself (including, perhaps, your own institution?) conducts so little systematic inquiry about its own effectiveness, and what you might do to correct or strengthen weaknesses that you find.

LIBERAL EDUCATION

There has been a small resurgence of interest in liberal education in recent years. More than interest needs to be stimulated. Substantial restoration (albeit with appropriate redefinition) needs to occur.

A successfully imparted liberal education is an absolutely essential component in the knowledge base of a teacher candidate. It provides the background and helps establish the context from which essential value decisions are made, goals are established, and the functions of education in a free society can be understood. It equips prospective teachers with the fundamental intellectual skills on the basis of which they can understand society, appreciate our culture and those of others, think and communicate effectively, and formulate a grounded sense of self in relation to the larger world. There is not a handful of college and university campuses where teachers are trained that would not benefit from intensive examination of the definitions of a liberal education for the last fifth of the twentieth century and how each proposes to deliver what it finally settles upon as its particular commitment.

Liberal education is only in minor part a distribution of courses across the traditional areas of the natural sciences and math, the behavioral and social sciences, and the arts and humnanities. The manner in which such courses are organized and taught and the aims that are thereby pursued by design, in fact, define liberal education. Achieving such ends cannot be accomplished by the teacher education faculty alone. The initiative must be endorsed and vigorously led by academic officers at the institutional level. Liberal education is part of the knowledge base for teacher education and must be provided for the advance contemplated in this essay to occur.

POST-BACCALAUREATE TEACHER EDUCATION

In the years ahead teacher education will almost certainly become a post-baccalaureate activity. Already extended programs are under development; they will almost certainly give way to post-baccalaureate programs of professional study to which liberal arts graduates with strong academic majors will be admitted, thereby addressing a central concern about the quality of incoming students to teacher education programs. Although this movement will come about because of the inexorable forces now working within the profession, the forces could be aided in all sorts of ways if college and university level leadership would begin to plan now for the transition. True, some institutions now authorized to train teachers will no longer do so, but since they will retain responsibility for the baccalaureate level training in liberal education and the academic major, they will still be deeply involved in the overall effort.

ADEQUATE RESOURCES FOR TEACHING AND INQUIRY

You could hardly expect to be reading a memo from an education dean, could you, without hearing a plea for resources. Here it is.

Teacher education has to become, uniformly and thoroughly, a clinically grounded professional training program. That means, among other things, that it must take place in specialized and field settings under conditions of close, continuous, and increasingly highly-mediated supervision. At the funding level permitted by the subsidy models followed in most public institutions until relatively recently, it has been only marginally possible to offer such programs. If you look at the subsidy models in your states or the comparative analysis of instructional resources allocated to the several academic programs under your charge, it will be quickly apparent what kinds of priority the education programs have had budgetarily and the extent to which there has been a willingness to support the clinical training model required for effective programs.

The teaching expectations of education faculty, particularly in the teacher training programs, have been heavy even if only marginally clinical. As a result, there has been neither time nor, in far too many places, the expectation that teacher education faculty would engage in research or scholarship. The expectations that have long been implicitly demanded of education faculty in respect to teaching have to be expanded, now, to include inquiry.

The inquiry and scholarly expectations must be more pointedly communicated. Furthermore, support of several different kinds must be provided to make it possible for existing faculty to grow in these new directions. The renewed demand for raised standards needs to be understood in terms of past neglect which occurred in far too many places; expectations of arts and sciences and other professional faculty were not applied equally to education faculty. The results were predictable. Part of the resources teacher education faculty require, therefore, is clear expectations untainted by prejudgment borne of lower status in the eyes of others.

UNWARRANTED STATUS HIERARCHIES

The last comment leads directly to another area where college and university presidents can contribute. The profession will **earn** a better standing by taking the steps proposed in this essay. It is also true that to the extent it is unfairly relegated to lower status owing to academic prejudice and bias, it is denied access to intellectual resources and higher quality students. Presidential leaders that recognize the importance of quality teacher education and higher education's complex responsibilities in this regard will help by challenging unwarranted bias within their own institutions even as they provide clear expectations for higher standards of performance.[1]

PARTNERSHIPS WITH THE PROFESSION

The contributions of higher education to the education profession will be achieved in partnership with State agencies, local schools, and the organized profession. Rather than seeing such partnerships as interference in the proper prerogatives of higher education, as some academic officials have,[2] that partnership ought to be entered into willingly.

The basis for the partnership, however, should be kept clear. What higher education has to contribute to lower education is its inquiry capacities and the fulfillment of its responsibilities effectively to train new generations of professionals. Higher education should not be seen as a free resource available for any manner of direct consultant or advisory input school districts may require. The service which higher education can deliver to schools is that which simultaneously supports the performance of its prime teaching and research responsibilities. Unfortunately, the strapped financial circumstance of much of public education has often led school districts to expect of other agencies the kind of charity the educational system as a whole has expected of its professionals.[3]

On the other hand, there are still many in higher education who interpret the legitimate interests of public and professional authority in defining educational standards as intrusions into the proper autonomy of higher education. Some of these external influences do represent real problems for higher education. The increasing tendency for ever smaller professional accrediting bodies to attempt to define both resource requirements and organizational arrangements can be burdensome and intrusive and bears careful watching. The view, however, that universities ought to be completely free to define their curricula according to their own dictates independently of State standards, for example, cannot be justified given the larger public responsibility for assuring qualifications for persons responsible for children and young adults in their charge by force of law.

HIGHER EDUCATION AS INSTRUCTIONAL MODEL

Teachers emerging from institutions of higher education have been exposed to sixteen years of instruction. The most effective instruction nationally is that which takes place in the lower grades. It gets progressively less effective the older the students get. John Goodlad demonstrates this conclusively in his recent study. Student assessments of the quality of instruction in higher education confirm the need for improvement.

Given the extremely limited range and middling quality of instructional models available throughout higher education (**including** the teacher education programs!), teacher preparation programs would have to be instructionally efficient to a super-professional degree successfuly to impart the techniques of improved practice. It would be easier to turn a dandelion patch into a putting green using a mower alone! More fundamental prior steps need to be taken. Improvement can come about in the instructional capacity of higher education through the application of instructional evaluation, design, and faculty development activities, if Presidents insist upon and support such initiatives. That the route to improvement is itself an institutional inquiry function doubles its power as an effective instrument to achieve the professional aims identified here.[4]

MEMO TWELVE[1]

To: Executive Director, American Educational Research Association (AERA)

AERA is a vibrant, efficiently operated, multi-faceted concern. Some 14,000 strong, it reaches widely throughout the Nation, not to mention its international connections.[2]

The proposals contained in Part One of this volume envision a substantial and greatly expanded role for educational research and development. AERA is the primary professional organization in this sector. It could contribute substantially to the achievement of the reconceptualization of the profession advanced in this essay.

BEHAVIORAL AND SOCIAL INQUIRY IN SUPPORT OF EDUCATION

The Association could very fruitfully devote a small study effort to the character of behavioral and social inquiry and the manner in which it contributes to educational practice and policy. This need not be a large enterprise, but it ought to be a continuing one. In a sense, this would be AERA's "research agenda" analogous to that called for in the memo to Executive Directors of the practitioner-based organizations. Such an effort would help to focus the members' attention on the character of their enterprise, guide the development of research training curricula, and help establish the foundations for the Association's continuing role in offering sound advice to the professional and policy leadership.

RELATIONS WITH PRACTITIONER-BASED ORGANIZATIONS

In recent years the Association has taken increasingly active steps to relate more closely to practitioner-based organizations. These steps should be encouraged and expanded. AERA should cooperate, principally through its divisional and special interest group structure, in the development of substantive research agendas and syntheses of research oriented to diverse practitioner groups. Increasingly, AERA should see such efforts as a continuing obligation/opportunity for its members.

RELATIONS WITH TEACHER EDUCATION

So-called special interest groups on teacher education and on teacher preparation curriculum do exist, but far closer connection ought to obtain between the entire research enterprise in education and the professional preparation function. Herewith two suggestions.

The Executive Director of the American Association of Colleges for Teacher Education could be designated an **ex officio** member of the principal governing body of AERA. Such a mechanism would assure direct connection and the presentation of the professional preparation perspective on matters where it would be appropriate.

Second, AERA's Organization of Institutional Affiliates (OIA) could contribute substantially to the work of the Association and the professional preparation function if its resources and energies could also be directed to the research related organizational and and administrative needs of the education professional leadership in higher education, especially.

At present the dominant orientation of AERA is toward the interests of its individual members. This is a tremendous strength which could be still further enhanced. OIA has increasingly brought to bear on AERA the concerns and perspectives of administrative figures within teacher preparation, research organizations, and a handful of local and State educational agencies. These influences are important and could become even more so if the Association could also find effective ways of capitalizing on organizational and functional perspectives that necessarily reach beyond the concerns of individuals. OIA constitutes a vehicle through which these kinds of contributions could be made to the research community as well as to the practitioner and policy communities.

In proposing greater attention to organizational perspectives relating to educational research and its purposes the intention is not to reallocate present energies so much as it is to make claims on additional commitments that might be brought to the Association and its purposes. Nonetheless, teacher education administrators are going to require conceptual and organizational help to increase the inquiry focus of their faculties and their programs, and AERA should be able to perform an important catalyst role.

THE IMPORTANCE OF AFFIRMATIVE ACTION IN THE RESEARCH ENTERPRISE

The multi-perspectival character of behavioral and social inquiry, its metaphorical richness, and its unavoidable connection to values makes it vitally important that the research community reflect the breadth of interests existing in the publics being served by the Nation's educating institutions. The Association has recognized its affirmative action responsibilities through policy statements and actions, its standing committee structure, as well as through the appointment of officers for this purpose in the Divisions. The importance of attending to affirmative action in the Association's activities owes not just to obligations not to deny access, but because of the important truth that what we know depends, in some measure, on "where we're coming from and where we're going." That requires assurance of the presence of diversity in active inquiry itself.

MEMO THIRTEEN

To: Executive Director
American Association of Colleges for Teachers Education (AACTE)

Signs of the dramatically increased teacher educator interest in inquiry and scholarship can be seen. The 1982 annual meeting was oriented to that theme. An AACTE Task Force on Inquiry was organized the objective of which was to formulate a set of recommendations to the Association on how best to undertake continuing attention to such concerns. These initiatives must be deepened and broadened.

THE INQUIRY TASK FORCE

During the past two years AACTE supported an Inquiry Task Force. Recently, a difficult decision was made to discontinue the group in favor of seeing to it that all the organized entities of AACTE sustained a focus on and commitment to the connection to inquiry. I would strongly urge the recreation of the Inquiry Task Force, if only to perform the task of "keeping honest" the other AACTE initiatives on this score.

LIAISON WITH THE RESEARCH COMMUNITY

AACTE needs to establish a more direct and continuous relationship to the research community. One way of accomplishing this would be to make the Executive Director of the American Educational Research Association an **ex officio** member of its Board of Directors. An inter-organizational connection of this kind would symbolize and create opportunities for direct communications between the two organizations that would complement the proposal to AERA that you as Executive Director of AACTE serve **ex officio** on AERA's governing body.

OVERCOMING FEARS, INCAPACITY, UNFAMILIARITY, AND OBJECTION

The uncertainties and anxieties in teacher education faculty and institutions about research, scholarship, and related inquiry activities and the requirements for change implicit in all of them are no secret to those familiar with the field. Approaching them constructively will have to be done supportively but unflinchingly.

Fears have arisen, for example, over the implications of arguments that the knowledge required of teachers strongly suggests that teacher education follow the baccalaureate program rather than be incorporated within it. Some colleges and universities long engaged in teacher education programs fear that no longer performing the certification function may affect their very survival. The Association should support study efforts to show why that fear is unwarranted and what steps can be taken or insisted upon to prevent unintended negative side effects.

Incapacity and lack of familiarity with inquiry ought not to be considered a permanent condition. After all, teacher educators believe in learning don't they, for themselves as well as for others? The Association would be well advised to assess teacher education's needs and desires in respect to inquiry and then provide mechanisms or incentives for creating the necessary capacity where it does not now exist. Building capacity for inquiry within teacher education in the face of both anxiety and unfamiliarity ought to be approached in two ways -- generically across the profession, probably drawing on professional associations like AACTE and the Association of Teacher Educators, as well as in terms of approaches that are uniquely tailored to given institutional settings.

Disagreement with the objective of grounding the profession on inquiry processes and products is another matter altogether. This cannot be ignored, for continuation in its present form will prove disabling in the long run to teacher education and to the larger profession. The Association should take positive steps to confront the controversy where it has been raised, unravel its elements, and learn what is really at issue and what is not, with the ultimate aim of arriving at a consensus view. The recommendation is easy to make. Achieving the goal will be something else. One of the reasons why is addressed below.

COPING WITH THE POLITICS OF TEACHER EDUCATION

Teacher education in America embraces a very broad range of institutions. Public and private (some church related), large and small, single purpose or multi-purpose, urban, rural and in between, baccalaureate, graduate, or both, almost exclusively oriented toward research or engaging in none at all. This array has organized itself in a variety of ways. But half the institutions training teachers belong to AACTE as you well know. Less than half submit themselves for accreditation by The National Council for the Accreditation of Teacher Education. Further subdivisions occur in the form of the Association of Independent Liberal Arts Colleges of Teacher Education (AILACTE), Teacher Education Council of State Colleges and Universities (TECSCU), and the Association of Colleges and Schools of Education in State Universities and Land Grant Colleges and Affiliated Private Universities (ACSESULGC/APU). Another smaller group of research-oriented universities has been operating for some years under the title of the Deans' Network. Individual teacher education faculty organize themselves through the Association of Teacher Educators (ATE). This organizational variety, overlapping sometimes but also leaving out significant numbers of institutions and teacher education faculty, frequently reflects strongly held differences of opinion about where to go and what to do in teacher education, to say nothing of education generally.[1]

The politics are complicated by virtue of the fact that the policy power in AACTE, the umbrella organization if there is any at all, bears little relation to the production realities of teacher education in America. While quantitative concerns may be of lesser interest in the final analysis, teacher education's ability to present a strong national consensus in terms of its goals is certainly complicated by the problems of adequately reflecting where the bulk of the nation's teachers are being trained. As in all voluntary professional organizations, however, responsibility does tend to gravitate to those with energy and ideas. The inquiry challenge, though, is one of the issues that divides institutions of teacher education. Small programs understandably feel threatened. Institutions whose faculty are not engaging in inquiry feel threatened. Both types constitute a very substantial majority of all the groups save for the smaller Deans' Network, TECSCU, and ACSESULGC.

As Executive Director you live with these real differences and play a vital balancing role between the competing pressures, but the long range advance of teacher education responsibilities rests on finding ways, finally, to work through the conflicts,[2] or face the prospect of either maintaining the present stalemate or running the more likely risk of watching forces external to the profession cut a swath through us. Teacher education has too much to contribute to American education and the Nation's well-being to permit draconian solutions minus our involvement.

Teacher education is not yet rearranging deck chairs, but our Titanic has received its radar warnings. As Executive Director you are in the unenviable position of forcing us to keep our eyes glued to the scope and reminding us where the steering wheel is as well as how it works!

MEMO FOURTEEN

To: State Boards of Education

You constitute the highest level of public authority exclusively concerned with the goals, structure, staffing, support, and operations of the public schools in your States. As you are sometimes painfully aware, other coordinate authorities -- the legislature, the Governor, the courts -- also have powers and responsibilities that directly affect what you can accomplish and how, but none has the prime, comprehensive, and continuous authority charged to you.

The inherent complexity of each State's elementary and secondary educational system and its necessary dependence on sectors beyond your immediate control (for example, higher education) delimits the freedom you have to act as the lead policy body. The transformation proposed here will ultimately require your endorsement in countless ways -- ratifying new certification standards, redefining school standards, altering the bases on which districts are subsidized, and so on. It will be speeded to the extent that you perceive its potential power and actively press for its introduction into schools of your State.

Like all engaged in the social services, competing interests and the plethora of agencies and actors make it very difficult, even for authorities with designated prime responsibility, to take a leadership position. When acting within the confines of a complex spider web, it is all the more difficult to contemplate the task of spinning a new one!

A State Board could find itself persuaded of the power of the idea and slowly and systematically act to stimulate the changes. You could work first through a rethinking of the preparation of school personnel. You could begin by calling for careful consideration by the professional leadership in your State of the underlying concepts of the organizing principle of inquiry. You could decide to wait until the professional leadership itself begins to come forth with proposals pointing toward this conception. All three postures are defensible, although, not surprisingly, the preferred one would be your assumption of active leadership.

Whatever route to your engagement in the ideas presented in this proposal, two of its dimensions are especially appropriate.

INSISTENCE ON THE QUALITY AND THOROUGHNESS OF SUPPORTING ARGUMENTS

Any policy body will want to feel that it is acting on the basis of good information, clear purpose, and sound rationales. As a lay body you are not in a position to gather information yourselves, but you can formulate clear purposes, and insist upon the presentation of good information and sound arguments. And of course you do that. In the present context, I would urge on you two criteria to employ in judging proposals for reform which come to you for consideration.

Comprehensiveness

A system as complex and interlinked as education makes it virtually certain that initiatives taken in one sector will have impacts on others. Policy initiatives presented to you should explore those cross impacts. They should be able to demonstrate the validity of their conclusions by affording representatives of all sectors opportunities to review and comment upon the analyses. Such an opportunity was followed when Ohio revised its program standards for teacher education following a policy process which deliberately engaged various stakeholder groups concurrently but with full information about the progress of each group being shared with all the others.

The criterion of comprehensiveness will do much to admit to consideration the interests of those representing the multiple perspectives that characterize effective formation of educational policy. In a sense it is an already obvious and normal occurrence in a field as intensely political as education, but it takes on new meaning in light of the exposition of the characteristics of educational inquiry explored in Part Two of this essay.

The Quality of the Argument

Just as important as access, however, is the quality of the argument and the documentation underpinning it. Again, an example may help. In several States, notably Virginia and California, policies have recently been adopted to open widely teacher certification. The idea is to permit liberal arts graduates with academic majors to teach with a minimal background in professional preparation provided there is some kind of mentoring arrangement with an experienced teacher. The proposal responds to complaints by academically qualified individuals that they are denied opportunities to make their skills available to young people unless they are first willing to complete certification requirements. From the perspective of a profession and its policy structure acting on the basis of knowledge, what issues required examination here?

1. Wholly apart from presumptions about the quality of (a) the curricular and instructional offerings in teacher preparation programs, (b) the institutions approved for certification purposes, and (c) the evaluation criteria and procedures employed to that end (responsibility for approval of all three is now vested in the State Educational Agency), what knowledge does a teacher require? To answer that question it is necessary to know the legal obligations falling on teachers, the characteristics of the students they are likely to encounter, the kinds of decisions teachers are called upon to make and actions they are required to take, the kinds of functions they must perform, and the nature of the organizational and authority structure within which they are called upon to perform their duties.

2. Given an understanding of those needs and responsibilities, does a liberal education and content mastery in an academic discipline provide adequate background? What is the evidence? On what basis is that argument drawn?

3. Is it possible to acquire those understandings through direct experience? What is the basis for that conclusion?

4. If direct experience needs to be supplemented by an apprenticeship model how exactly is **apprenticeship** defined? How much support is to be provided, how close, how intense, supplied by whom, and at what cost? How does the proposed apprenticeship compare to those provided in fields employing apprenticeship training models?

5. What is the basis for believing that opening certification to individuals without formal training in human learning, curriculum planning and design, handicapping conditions, testing and measurement, classroom management, diagnostic and prescriptive instruction, multi-factored assessment, or awareness of cultural differences and their impact on the environment and aims of schooling will improve education and not generate negative influences and outcomes? How will teachers who have been trained in and know such things be able to work, in the long run, with those who do not?

These questions, answers to which ought to be required before undertaking radical revisions of existing policies, are not meant to deny either the problems that exist or the frustrations that have mounted in the face of those problems. The questions do address the fundamental issue whether teaching is an occupation best served by talented amateurs or by individuals well-trained to perform a complex professional role. We might even acknowledge the certainty that a small percentage of gifted "naturals," through energy, charisma, and the wise selection of the schools within which they choose to work, might be superbly successful. After admitting that 3 percent to teaching, how about the other 97 percent? How will children and the public be assured that those in the far larger portion will know what they are doing?

I have treated the example extensively because it speaks to the heart of the proposition advanced in this volume. There is too much at stake for us to act on mere prejudice, bias, or frustration, attitudes perhaps with some foundation, but in the long run unlikely to generate productive outcomes. Returning teaching to a social function performed by amateurs is not the direction we should be taking. On the other hand, continuation of intellectually and professionally weak, ill conceived, low standard, and inadequately staffed preparation programs cannot be permitted either. Systematic inquiry, solid evidence, sound knowledge, and justifiable rationales will always be bases for responsible action.

POLICY LEADERSHIP AND PROFESSIONAL AUTONOMY

As noted elsewhere, increasing professional capacity and instructional power will be accompanied by legitimate claims for greater autonomy on the part of teachers. There will be little point in functioning in an inquiry mode if it is not possible to act on the results, either because of elaborate constraints or because of frequent intrusions by policy officials in the decisions and actions of teaching staff.

Tensions will always exist between policy leadership and the professional staff in educational institutions. Nothing that could be said here could hope to eliminate them. On the other hand, the nature of those tensions is likely to change quite significantly. The proper assignment of domains of professional autonomy will require careful consideration by policy leadership at the State and local level.

Once schools become hierarchically organized in the sense described in Part One, one of the real impediments to legitimate professional status -- the isolation of practitioners from one another which prevents the application of common professional standards -- would thus be removed. Professional standards are not principally upheld by ethics committees or professional standards boards except, in the final analysis, for the most extreme cases of violation. Rather, it is the day-to-day collaboration that reminds, provides opportunities to correct, and maintains the climate and expectations of professional performance. Thus, an important precondition for professional performance will have been created.

How much autonomy will those hierarchically structured teams of teachers have in the specific design and delivery of curriculum and instruction? One likely response from policy levels like yours is pressure for clearer specification of performance outcomes of schooling. These need not be exclusively in academic achievement terms because that is but one of several important areas of public demand. Once the aims are more clearly specified, however, teams of professionals would be expected to accomplish those ends fully utilizing the resources at their command (including one another). Indeed, the organized profession in an **entire district** might come to be held acountable for effective performance once the implications of a professionalized operation in service of the public began to become clear. One could imagine a very different kind of collective bargaining beginning to include drawing specifications for the definition of effective service expected of the profession as well as for the conditions and terms of employment. Defining what such provisions might mean and how professional organizations might be held accountable for them is an activity that might engage the enthusiastic participation of higher education **and** the organized profession.

At the present time fractionalized and bureaucratic structures of schooling hold few incentives for the kind of collaborative performance envisaged. Once collaborative performance begins to occur the relations between boards as policy definers and practitioners as professionals organizing themselves to achieve those policy aims should alter significantly to the benefit of those whom the schools seek to serve.

MEMO FIFTEEN

To: Members of Congress

The increase in the effectiveness of the service of professional educators projected in this volume cannot be achieved without the participation of the Congress of the United States. The notion that the national interest in education can be served by relying solely on the States and localities is certainly not true in the present instance.

THE IMPORTANCE OF FEDERAL SUPPORT FOR INQUIRY

Adequate resources for formal inquiry and related activities in support of the educational institutions of the Nation will never be available from individual universities, local school districts, or State educational agencies. Their closeness to the immediate demands and desires of those they serve, plus their direct proximity to those who are paying the overwhelming share of the cost, lead responsible administrators of those agencies and institutions to give higher priority to claims for direct service over requests for research dollars. Such judgments reflect a reality few would question. Still, these decisions have sharply delimited the work that has been done and the accomplishments derived from it. It might be possible for individual schools to conduct their activities more from an inquiry frame of mind, but there will be little opportunity for significant advance in our ideas about learning, teaching, the functions and limits of schooling, or its organization and support, and virtually no opportunity for undertaking the crucial development functions, if support is not forthcoming at the Federal level.

Any United States Senator or Representative who has had the tenacity to read this far (or who just turned to this section!) might well ask why any further claims against the public purse ought to be made by the proponents of educational research and development. After all, if educational research had been doing what it was supposed to be (as one of your colleagues argued ten years ago), we wouldn't be in the mess we are! Why give it any more?

WHY INCREASE APPROPRIATIONS FOR EDUCATIONAL INQUIRY?

The question is respectable. Its answer lies in two directions. One focuses, once again, on the nature of behavioral and social inquiry and what real benefits it can hope to impart. The second compares the views of legislators on matters of educational policy (which more nearly approximate those of the ultimate clients of schools -- individuals, the greater body politic, and the economic sector) with the understandings derived from formal inquiry.

Social science is inherently disturbing because it tends, in the short run at least, to increase conflict rather than resolve it. It does so by sharpening policymakers' attention to more factors than they might otherwise wish to be aware of, by displaying the complexity of the phenomena under study, and by giving voice to the real and different perspectives present. In many respects, policy makers might wish they -- that is, social scientists -- would go away. But policy makers somewhat reluctantly avoid acting on that wish overtly because they know they must know; with all its difficulties, the results of rigorous formal inquiry by social scientists must be part of what policy makers work with as policy and practice are addressed. The covert response, however, is to keep the funding small. Still, without behavioral and social inquiry we are reduced to sheer opinion, habit, and the particular collections of experience represented by the members of the group at hand.

There have been few champions of behavioral and social inquiry in the Congress. There have been far many more critics. And there are legions of skeptics. Perceptions of small payoff are partly to blame (but the chicken/egg problem of scale of effort given complexity of the task must be mentioned in the same breath). Persistent criticisms from within the ranks of the research community itself about topics funded, approaches taken, and support mechanisms employed must give many of you pause. (On the other hand, in a field with so much to do, so few to do it, so high expectations, and so few resources, any decision made at all must be right and wrong at the same time because of the scope of competing demands and the paucity of resources to satisfy any but a minute portion.)

Elitist images projected by some supporters of behavioral and social inquiry have also been to blame. Pyramidical views of science, perhaps appropriate in other fields but clearly less so in the social sciences, have given rise to the view that only "the best" should be funded. Surely, only competent work ought to be supported, but claims that only the highest quality work ought to be supported conveniently ignores how such judgments can be made and on what criteria. There are fundamental issues here given the unavoidability of value connections in social science reserarch and the existence of divergent views of what it means to know as, for example, between academics, practitioner educators, and the clients of schools.

Does this mean there are no firm answers? And if it does, why then support educational research and development?

What it means is that there are no **single** answers to the difficult puzzles of human behavior. There **are** multiple views; anytime a single view is proffered, great caution should be exhibited. Indeed, the "knowing" about social phenomena does not begin to be complete at any point in time until many perspectives, academic and other, have been brought to bear. C. Wright Mills said many years ago that the two great generalizations of social science are multiple causation and probability. There is always more than one reason and and there are no sure things. The crucial question is whether we can afford any longer to act in the social sector, generally, but in education in particular, without providing ample opportunity for rigorously understanding those many reasons, what the dimensions of that probability are, and why they exist as they do.

The irony of the low level of support, of course, is that the burden on educational and social science research is heavier at the same time that resources are vastly smaller. The popular view is that the resources are smaller because these sciences are less rigorous, less mature, and, therefore, less deserving. On the contrary, these sciences are not less rigorous; they are more difficult. They are not less sophisticated or mature, but complicated by the interventions of values, time, and human consciousness. **The truly "hard" sciences are those that study humankind!**

Seeking substantially increased appropriations for research and development at the Federal level is directed only to the narrower sector of education conducting formal inquiry (research) and the more expensive development responsibility, functions which will not be undertaken as a normal part of the effort of schools, colleges, and universities. This essay, of course, has advanced an even more comprehensive role for inquiry in a redefined profession of education, but the Federal role in supporting such a movement should be limited to the research and development sector **per se, not** the subsidization of practice-based inquiry itself.

There is a final set of reasons why appropriations need to be increased for educational research. Those reasons have to do with the consequences of the combination of the "political" character of educational research (that is, the unavoidability of its touching on values issues) and the fact that education in America is politically **organized** as well.

Consider the following parallel. There are fifty State legislatures in America. Very rarely, however, do we hear anyone propose that it would be more efficient to refer to the Congress matters now dealt with in Albany, Columbus, Sacramento, or Tallahassee or, conversely, that the legislative investigation undertaken in Richmond would satisfy State Senators in Cheyenne. Certainly part of what is operating here is a less defensible so-called "n.i.h." factor (if it's "not invented here," it's not acceptable). But there is a more basic consideration. Effective education systems work because they forge partnerships with their clients; that means closely tailoring educational programs and instruction to their needs and aspirations. That cannot be done without careful consideration of the unique client characteristics and educational aspirations at the local and State level. The requirements of Virginia are not necessarily those of Idaho; what might match the "style" of a community in Oregon might grate transplanted to Connecticut. Arguments against duplication of effort, therefore, are not so much wrong as misplaced; effectiveness and appropriateness come much closer to the mark. Given the political organization of schooling and the broad political purposes it is designed to serve, supporting inquiry processes to serve multiple perspectives throughout the institutions of instruction is essential.

LEGISLATIVE REQUIREMENTS

No changes are required in the basic authority present in the legislation under which the National Institute of Education and the vocational and handicapped research progams are conducted. One desirable change would be to increase the accountability of NIE to the Congress by clarifying the responsibilities of the National Council for Educational Research (NCER). The officials responsible for operating NIE's programs and defending them before appropriation and legislative oversight committees ought to be one and the same. Present authority, however, empowers the NCER to make policy for the Institute which the Director is responsible for carrying out. When one considers that the NIE Director also reports to the Secretary (through an Assistant Secretary) the line of accountability becomes even more blurred. Congress should redraft the legislation so that the officials responsible for administering NIE's programs and representing them to the Congress for appropriation requests and legislative oversight purposes are also the ones with policy authority.

Given the Federal structure of education in America, a strong advisory apparatus is essential. Furthermore, given the nature of behavioral and social inquiry, it is probably desirable that only a relatively limited number of decisions be made by the NIE staff. In the main, NIE's decision making ought to be limited to the creation of mechanisms for providing support, with specific judgments on work to be done being made by panels and advisory groups broadly reprsentative of the profession and its clients. When NIE's legislative authorization is renewed, the NCER should be made advisory to the director, and the terms of its members defined and staggered to provide for continuity and stability. Serious consideration ought to be given to establishing an 18-member Council, six of whom are appointed every other year to a six-year, non-renewable term of appointment.

ACCOUNTABILITY OF NIE TO THE CONGRESS

Aside from the one technical adjustment in legislative authority, the principal Congressional role should be monitoring the manner in which NIE conceives of its long-range responsibilities. The primary focus should be on how NIE views inquiry in support of the improvement of educational practice and how it meets its obligations to provide for the maintenance and enhancement of the system supporting research and development for education.

More specifically, Congress should review and monitor initiatives forthcoming from NIE like those proposed in the recommendations to the Director. Those recommendations speak to increasing the orientation to inquiry of institutions preparing educational personnel and the support of design studies of inquiry-based school organizations. They endorse serious effort directed to sustaining and strengthening the system for educational research and development. They seek clarification of decision-making roles for educational research given that the Institute operates within a Federally-structured educational system. They call for long-range planning, more synthesizing reviews of knowledge for practitioners and others, and the maintenance and expansion of the regional educational laboratory and research and development center programs. These recommendations provide a framework within which Congress should plan, slowly and, later, substantially, to increase the resources for support of educational research and development. The overall aim is an increasingly effective professional system of education more closely attuned in its sophistication and accomplishment to the needs of the twenty-first century.

A CONCLUDING NOTE

In Chapter Two where various impediments to grounding teaching and the profession of education on inquiry processes and products were discussed, I commented on my own observations of legislative and political figures confronting the work of social scientists. I noted that the reactions were often skeptical or worse and I attributed that to fundamentally different perspectives of what it means "to know." Because the issue of orientation toward and definition of knowledge is so important, I want to close this communication to you with a brief return to that observation.

Social scientists look at the world through frames of reference which are different from those of either practitioners or laypersons (including legislators). When none of the aforementioned are aware of the equal legitimacy of the interpretations of reality presented by the others or, worse, the different contributions made by one are actually disvalued by another, then we truly have "trouble in River City."

Laypersons live with complexity and, for the most part, they succeed tolerably well in their confrontations with it. Scholars try to find conceptually rigorous pathways through that complexity, seeking to understand one or another aspect with sophistication and elegance. In doing so, their research techniques and special language often come across as increasing complexity still further or uselessly abstracting phenomena from reality. Academics, educators, and clients do encounter the world of educational practice and accomplishment with different orientations. Those orientations can support one another if only each would give due credence to the others. When all of us within the profession together with those having policy responsibility become comfortable with those two ideas, then a major enabling step will have been taken to the improvement of educational practice through systematic inquiry.

Part Four

RESTATEMENT AND REJOINDERS

CHAPTER NINE   REPRISE, PROSPECTIVE COUNTER ARGUMENTS, AND A RESTATEMENT OF THE STAKES AND THE PROMISE

Resurgent interest in the challenges presented by American education has the popular press busy, political leadership engaged, and the professional education community wondering, in some measure, what is going to happen next. Governors, state legislatures, and State Boards of Education have been pressured to act and in numerous instances have done so with unprecedented haste and comprehensiveness.

Unfortunately, even as the renewed attention is opening possibilities for action that could not have existed without it, much that has been proposed has responded to symptoms rather than causes. It has been excessively particularlistic in its orientation, and sometimes almost embarassingly mushy-headed.

THE PROPOSAL RESTATED

This volume has proposed a quite different and more fundamental approach to the same questions being raised across the land. It has sought to address causes underlying the present dissatisfaction by offering a conceptualization of how the profession might come to act in the future if it organized itself upon a single over-riding principle: **Teaching must come to rest on the processes and products of inquiry. Furthermore, we in the profession must come to understand that inquiry is not solely something done elsewhere in the university, research center, or laboratory, but is a vital frame of reference that should guide and inform our day-to-day responsibilities as practitioners and policy makers.** Inquiry activities undertaken, whether directed to theoretical concerns or the world of practice, must recognize fully the unique characteristics of the behavioral and social phenomena to which they were directed. A concomitant development sees a restructuring of teaching to end the nearly total isolation of the professional lives of teachers and building-level administrators in lower education and the isolation of faculty in their teaching functions in higher education.

Those who have always thought teaching ought to be a reflective activity will not find anything exceptional about the proposal; what is exceptional is that we do not train teachers or administrators with expectations for such activity, we do not structure schools on the assumption it must take place, nor is the system as a whole supported by a parallel, directly linked research and development enterprise of a scale that would be useful.

The implications of acting on inquiry processes and products are many. They bear on theoretical knowledge and the tested innovations of educational development. They affect how teachers view the fine-grain information about their students (and their students' progress) and the use of such information to support the important responsibilities for curricular and instructional design in the classroom. Teacher education must become a post-baccalaureate professional training program. Schools must be organized into 7-10 member hierarchically-structured teams responsible for 200-250 children each, led by a senior or lead teacher with advanced training. Acting through the greater autonomy justified by their greater capacity, teachers would be expected to organize into effective instructional units, effective defined in terms of the scope and breadth of their achievement measured against the stated policy goals of school districts. Additional costs, above those required anyway because of the uncompetitive salary levels now accorded teachers, are estimated in the 10% range, including the increment required to recognize the greater responsibility of the lead teacher, the increased investment in teacher education and materials costs for teaching teams, and the expansion of the research and development system in support of education.

The proposal relates the accomplishments of the profession closer to the aspirations of its many stakeholders. It stimulates a unification of the now disparate elements of the profession. Finally, it contributes directly to the purposes of a free society by calling for the design of schools which model in their day-to-day behavior the kinds of activities ordinary citizens might be expected to undertake as they confront their lives, their society, and the maintenance and enhancement of the republic.

Any successful proposal for educational reform in America will require the coordinate efforts of vast numbers of different kinds of officials and professionals. We do not have a National Ministry of Education nor would we want one. No czar is available to decree a cohesive set of steps to be taken. No conducter exists to wave a baton commanding the simultaneous attention of flautists, tympani, first violin, and horn. **If the kind of fundamental change required is to be undertaken and achieved it will take independent action by many according to a common theme on which broad agreement exists.** This essay has sought to sketch out such a theme and suggest the kinds of differentiated yet harmonious actions that diverse actors might choose to take. As simply put as possible, it is a theme which defines professional educators as persons who in the context of formal schooling **know**:

> **how** to do something,
> **why** they are doing it,
> **that** they are doing it when they are,
> whether they **should** be doing it,
> when to **stop** doing it,
> when they **don't** know, and, finally,
> reasonable strategies to **determine** what to do **anyway**!

The theme guiding the route to reform suggested in this volume is that **the** essential query for professional educators is "Do we know what we're doing and why?" When we ask it, we are engaging in inquiry. When we are challenged by others who ask it, we are being subjected to inquiry. When we act as a profession daily and moment by moment according to its requirements, then we will be grounded on inquiry.

COUNTER ARGUMENTS

When proposing educational reform, it pays to harbor few illusions. There will be objections raised from a number of quarters on a variety of competing premises. A few can be anticipated and ought to be briefly addressed.

Some will object by saying that the absolutely **last** thing American education needs is further development of the "professionalization of teaching." (It is hard to write that criticism without hearing the curled lip with which it so often uttered.) Others will express incredulity that a proposal could be so naive as to believe that the behavioral and social sciences have anything -- or that much -- to contribute, a posture whose adherents vary in their degree of genuine doubt or unvarnished prejudice. A third class of objections will come from those genuinely convinced that curricular content is everything, and pedagogy a matter of such lesser interest and importance as to be unworthy time and attention. A fourth will doubt our capacity to undertake reform on the scope and scale proposed here.

Rejection of Professionalization

The reservations arising from this concern take two forms. One is the perception that the organized profession has used its powers to serve itself at the expense of its clients, and that in recent years its focus on political power has diminished its legitimacy and credibility as a truly professional enterprise. The accuracy of that perception can be argued; what is important is its existence. The second form is the widespread experience of parents who find many teachers and administrators bureaucratic, system maintaining, less than caring, unwilling to help, and resistant to being held accountable for their performance. The picture is a stereotype; like many stereotypes it rests on substantial regularities. The unfairness of the generalization applied to the majority takes nothing away from its truth; anyone correctly described in terms of the stereotype sketched above ought not to be working with children in schools.

The perception that professionalization has succeeded in distancing teachers from those they serve[1] and encouraged teachers to pursue their own self-interest at the expense of others' ought not to be confused, however, with the ideas advanced here. The justification for the proposal to ground the profession on inquiry points in two directions simultaneously; acting on the basis of knowledge will improve the effectiveness of teaching and the schools, but it will at the same time create a climate among the teachers far more intellectually stimulating than obtains at present. Continuous examination of accomplishments against aims and the collaborative redirection of effort by teams of teachers working together is a quite different picture from the perceptions which fuel the objection.

The underlying assumption is that most teachers want to function as professionals. Most reject the narrow definitions of purpose implied in the stereotype, even as they might acknowledge that the low status they have been accorded by the public has inexorably moved some teachers and some of their organizations to follow narrow or defensive courses of action others might eschew.

Those unhappy with the present situation and who ascribe responsibility for it to the hopeless quality and self-interestedness of the teacher training establishment and the organized profession suggest an alternative to sound professionalization; they would introduce talented amateurs into the schools. This solution, however, does nothing to address the root causes of lesser talent to be found in inadequate salaries and a professionally unrewarding work environment. Furthermore, how the introduction of small numbers of essentially unprepared though well-meaning individuals will have substantial positive impact over the long haul without a fundamental re-thinking of the sort proposed here, remains a mystery.

Doubts Over the Power of Social Science

The sub-heading is, perhaps, overly polite. Evidence of skepticism over the fruitfulness of advances growing from social science may be found everywhere.[2]

Some of that doubt is entirely justified. The basis for the doubt has much to do, however, with the scale of the enterprise to date and, especially, the failure to invest more than minimally in the crucial development and practice-directed inquiry activities.

A more frustrating kind of rejection, however, comes at the hands of those who misunderstand or fear systematic examination of social phenomena or who are simply irrationally prejudiced against it. In recent months there has been considerable evidence of these kinds of sentiments abroad in the land. Some arise from ignorance about the nature of social science. Some of it is more vindictive, flowing from narrow partisan considerations. Some of it is old-fashioned bias, the kind, for example, that leads to such rhetoric as "liberal mumbo jumbo of teachers' college theorists run amok" or references to "dashes of anthropological relativism" or the explicit rejection of the worth of pedagogical studies.[3] How to respond to this particular manifestation of twentieth century know-nothingism is less easy to determine than labeling it for what it is, but it represents a substantial hurdle. Argument will not be persuasive with such people; they are beyond being reached in that fashion. It will be necessary to consider them all "from Missouri"; only actions and accomplishments may succeed in reducing the contempt now so freely expressed.

A last concern, less an objection than a legitimate fear, is that proposals to reform education on the basis of inquiry systematically applied has what some of my colleagues call a "technicist" flaw. They ask me to consider what it would be like to found a profession not on **knowledge** but on **insight**, not on **certainty** but on **judgment**. Those who espouse this view remind us that knowledge will not safeguard against bad practice unless it contributes to judgment and self-understanding. In developing the ideas contained herein I have tried to encompass their concerns (I hope successfully, but I know they will tell me if not). Hence the insistent focus on inquiry as a process even more than the data or knowledge products. Hence the focus on multiple perspectives and different epistemologies. Hence the inclusion of the arts and humanities as ways of knowing and learning along with the more analytical frames of reference afforded by the behavioral and social sciences. Those who urge caution on me espouse a real concern here, one intimately connected to the ultimate purposes of education which, after all, seeks not only to produce effective parents, wage-earners, and citizens but to enable those who seek and receive it to define and extend once more what it means to be human.

Content Imperialists

A third source of counter arguments will be the view that the answer to educational reform lies in re-asserting standards by restoring real content to the curriculum. This group overlaps substantially with those who rail against the worth of pedagogy. But they also make an important and valid point -- there isn't much use in watered-down learning or a curriculum that does not connect students to the essence of our past and present. The problems with the assertion of the importance of content alone are that it presumes the same value frame as the person choosing the content, it tends to focus more or less exclusively on academic content which is certainly important but not everything, it virtually ignores critically important differences in learning ability, style, and context, and it speaks almost not at all to by far the greater portion of the root causes identified in Chapter One.

Actually, the proposed reformation of teaching advanced here presumes and insists on rigorous content. Content mastery **is** part of a teacher's knowledge base. Without it curriculum cannot be designed or delivered, student performance cannot be assessed, and the broader purposes of education cannot be achieved.

Is The Scale of the Proposal Too Great?

Concern is sure to be raised about the scale of the proposal. Too many different agencies, imperfectly relating to one another, embracing far too many professional roles, with no over-arching coordination mechanism makes the goal too difficult to achieve. It is a legitimate concern, but there are rejoinders.

First, the inquiry principle is capable of being acted upon by individuals wherever they happen to be in the system. Inquiry does not require orchestration. It constitutes a radically decentralized frame of reference. To the extent that anyone in the larger system resolutely functions on the basis of the processes and products of inquiry, over the long haul, the basic character of the enterprise will move in desired directions. There are, of course, key figures whose actions and authority reach beyond their immediate settings. Independent initiatives there can have substantial effects, even if coordinate authority structures are beyond their immediate control.

The viability of the proposal by virtue of its broadly democratic character -- i.e., actions in tune with it can be taken by literally millions of individuals by simply deciding to function that way -- is further complemented by the time frame within which it is presented. Achieving its ends will take decades. Viewed in the perspective of twenty, thirty, or forty years -- unusual, to say the least, in this era of expectations for instantaneous effects -- the probability of being able to achieve the proposed transformation increases dramatically.

Consider the following historical example. Before the beginning of the 19th century there were but five medical schools in America. Training proceeded according to an apprenticeship model. Success, therefore, depended on the master. A library was important and so was a hospital. The system of medical training gradually evolved, however, into a proprietary one, with local medical societies or groups of doctors organizing a typically two-year course as a business venture. While we now think of medical education as a four year course, medical historian Saul Benison wryly notes that the first four-year medical course in America was the War Between the States.

The first steps at reform were taken virtually at the same time in two places in America, at Harvard, under the leadership of Charles W. Eliot, and at Johns Hopkins under Daniel Coit Gilman. Harvard's Eliot moved to take the very successful proprietary medical college under the wing of the University. He sought a graded medical curriculum, finally getting what he wanted after a two year struggle. It would be twenty years, however, before Harvard expanded its two-year program to three. It was **twenty-five** before students stopped observing experiments in clinical ampitheaters and began performing them. In the 1890's Harvard succeeded in having all its students present baccalaureate degrees at entry, but even under President Lowell, who succeeded Eliot in 1909, arguments persisted that two years college work would be enough.

At Johns Hopkins the pattern of reformation in medical education was somewhat different. There the key was the hospital and the man who founded it, John Shaw Billings. Billings was one of the physicians who received his most important training at "Civil War Medical College." After the war he joined the Surgeon General's office and undertook the task of upgrading military hospitals. He also upgraded the library of the Surgeon General's office, transforming it into a master catalog and a device for transmitting knowledge in the fashion of an index medica. The library was a major step toward standardizing medical knowledge and the creation of handbooks that characterize developed professions.

Gilman hired Billings in the 1870's to plan the Johns Hopkins Hospital, the necessary precursor to the medical school Gilman envisioned for his university. The hospital opened and operated well before the medical school selected its first students, each of whom would require the possession of a Bachelor's Degree. All the degree candidates were schooled in the sciences by faculty members, many of whom had been trained at the great European universities. A key distinguishing feature of both the Harvard and the Johns Hopkins approaches was that medical faculty were not only engaged in the transmission of clinical knowledge and skill, but were also deeply engaged in the production of medical knowledge at the same time.

Thus it was that over a hundred years ago, Charles W. Eliot and Daniel Coit Gilman set about the reform of medical education in the United States. Their reasoning was analogous to that proposed here in respect to teacher education. They decided to create programs of medical education (a) founded on the extant and developing knowledge of the biological sciences, (b) committed to inquiry in the conduct of medical education, and (c) connected to a hospital under the control of the teaching faculty. Instead of accepting students with a high school diploma, they insisted on a baccalaureate degree. Instead of a two-year program, they insisted on four.

Thirty-four years later, when Abraham Flexner undertook a rating of the medical schools in North America, most of which were still operating on the post high school, two-year training model, he used Johns Hopkins as the model. Even so, it was another 20 years before the baccalaureate entry requirement and the four-year program became universal.

This brief excursion into history has several messages. It shows the power of a guiding image. It underscores the importance of individual effort and commitment. In the twentieth century context, even as it may make more than a few administrators feel somewhat wistful about the powers and prerogatives of executive leadership in 19th century American higher education, it reminds us of the importance of leadership and position in accomplishing largescale aims.

Hindsight is powerful but it can also be misleading. The purpose behind offering the example is certainly not to suggest that the transformation sought for education should use for its specifics those that were applied in medicine. The nature of the enterprise and the characteristics of the underpinning inquiry are fundamentally different as the chapters in Parts One and Two make clear. The **only** purpose in citing the example is to illustrate the worth of a multi-decade perspective and an organizing principle in approaching a transformation as fundamental and far-reaching as the one proposed.

ARE THERE REALLY ANY ALTERNATIVES?

The question appears to contradict a key notion stressed in this essay that one of the main contributions of behavioral and social inquiry to educational practice is awareness of multiple perspectives. Surely there must be more than one route to improving the educational systems of the Nation. Of course there are. For example, one could imagine an attempt to redefine the qualifications of teachers, give all teachers three to five years to demonstrate they embody those qualifications, fire the ones that don't, and replace them with persons who met the new standards. For obvious political and human reasons, the likelihood of such an approach ever actually occurring approaches zero.

How will increasing salaries across the board change anything save the important teacher morale variable? If the present staff are the problem, how will touching salaries make a difference?

None of the merit-pay/master-teacher proposals have yet been formulated adequately, although installing them anywhere might prove to be an important precedent in the establishment of differential pay schemes which then might come to be justified more firmly, after the fact, by moving in the direction of the proposals advanced here. Most of the merit pay proposals advanced have all the lure of the obvious with none of the substance of solution to the difficult problems of defining criteria, establishing credible procedures for applying them, assuring access of every deserving teacher to the indicated rewards (i.e. no arbitrary quotas as to the number of awards), and guaranteeing that merit awards do not come in lieu of addressing the basic salary grievances that exist.

The master teacher proposals have the same shortcomings. There has been little definition of what a master teacher is, how one would choose one, and only slightly more definition of what their duties might be. Conceptually, there are serious problems as well. The implication of much of the discussion about master teachers is that teaching is an art form, that master teachers can be recognized but not created, that the route to their emergence is essentially personal experience mediated by a capable practitioner. Insofar as the concept of master teacher denies the importance of theoretical knowledge and inquiry skills, it represents little progress at all and it may actually have negative consequences by deluding us into thinking we are adopting a constructive response. The jury is still out on the master teacher notion; it would have to be since the bill of particulars has yet to be presented. Suffice it to say here, however, that implicit in the master teacher notion is the idea that good teaching can be imparted through apprenticeship. The idea is virtually impossible to contest; the same is true in virtually every other profession as well. What we in education need to ask ourselves, however, is why we have nowhere adopted an apprenticeship training model that even begins to approach the length and intensity of the effective apprenticeship training programs of the trades and the arts. Of course teaching is an art. Of course apprenticeship, both pre- and in-service, would be effective. But teaching is more than a performing art. Formal knowledge and inquiry skills are also necessary and are not likely to be acquired through apprenticeship training models even if deployed with sufficient time and intensity.

Proposals for increasing the length of the school year and the school day and for more homework are not wrong in themselves. They would be very costly, however, and they ignore the essential need to examine what is done within the time frames available to teachers and children **now**. They have the additional disadvantage of implying that responsibility lies with the clients rather than with the system. This last is a message that applies insufficient pressure on the profession to learn to function in more effective ways.

THE PROMISE

The achievements of children **and** schools can be very substantially increased. Educational practice can be very greatly improved. Schools can be organized to become more intellectually rewarding places to work and to provide career paths to attract and keep the best and most intellectually able teachers in teaching. Instead of being a limiting factor on the Nation's ability to meet the technological, natural resource, and world citizenship responsibilities to which our children fall heir, America's schools, colleges, and universities can become the instruments by which we can seize and fully realize our opportunities.

Just suppose that our schools and colleges were able to improve their annual effectiveness with those seeking their services by a paltry one percent a year as measured by that most narrow criterion of any test scores one might care to name. Over the life of a child's tenure in school, that would increase her scores by more than **twelve percent**. Throw in the college years and the achievement gain would be more than **seventeen percent**. Such gains, even in the narrow terms suggested here, would be simply enormous!

An educational system, designed to rest on a firm and growing knowledge base about learning and instruction, staffed by teachers trained fully in its terms and in inquiry skills associated with the technical as well as philosophical dimensions of their tasks, and operating daily to adjust its functions on the basis of systematically observed effects of its own performance would be able to accomplish such a goal and more.

If we began now, the development of a reflective, self-analytical, self-correcting set of educational institutions would preclude the need to launch the commissions of 2003 to examine why the energies expended twenty years earlier bore so little lasting fruit. Knowledgeable politicians and policy analysts give the head of steam generated over educational reform barely eighteen months to work its effects; seven of those are already expended. The proposals in this essay provide the framework for reform. They have the additional virtue of constituting a frame of reference within which those charged with responsibility for the profession itself can continue the processes of transformation even when the extraordinary public focus begins to subside as it inevitably must.

If we began now, by the turn of the century we could be well on our way to creating a knowledge and inquiry based system of educating institutions offering more effective service to the Nation. Can we afford not to try?

NOTES

NOTES

Foreword

1. Increasing the Research Capacity of Schools of Education: a Policy Inquiry, School of Education, Oregon State University, March, 1981 (Partially supported under NIE Contract # NIE-G-80-G-80-0161).
2. Especially Jeffrey Bailey, Sandra Wittstein, Norita Aplin, Tony Birckhead, Mary Witham, and Gwendolyn Wooddell.

Introduction

1. A Nation at Risk: The Imperative of Educational Reform, The National Commission on Excellence in Education, U.S. Government Printing Office, Washington, D.C. 1983, No. 065-000-00177-2.
2. Principal among the many reports are: John I. Goodlad, A Place Called School, McGraw-Hill Book Company, 1983; Ernest L. Boyer, High School, Harper & Row Publishers, 1983; C. Emily Feistritzer, The Condition of Teaching - A State by State Analysis, The Carnegie Foundation for the Advancement of Teaching, 1983; The National Science Board Commission on Precollege Education in Mathematics, Science and Technology, Educating Americans for the 21st Century, National Science Foundation, 1983, CPCE-NSF-03; Feistritzer Associates, The American Teacher, Washington, D.C. 1983; The National Task Force on Education for Economic Growth, Action for Excellence, Education Commission of the States, Denver, Colorado, 1983; The Education EQuality Project, Academic Preparation for College, The College Board, New York, 1983; The Twentieth Century Fund Task Force on Federal Elementary and Secondary Education Policy, Making the Grade, New York, 1983; Carnegie Corporation, Education and Economic Progress: Toward a National Education Policy, New York, 1983; Mortimer Adler, The Paideia Proposal: An Educational Manifesto, Macmillan Publishers, New York, 1982; The Task Force on Higher Education and the Schools, The Need for Quality, Southern Regional Education Board, 1983; Merit Pay Task Force Report, Committee on Education and Labor, House of Representatives, October, 1983; A Study of High Schools, The National Association of Secondary School Principals and the Commission on Educational Issues, Theodore Sizer, Chairman (forthcoming); Redefining General Education in the American High School, The Association for Supervision and Curriculum Development (forthcoming); Gerald Grant, "Good Schools Project," Syracuse University (forthcoming); and Myron Atkin and Donald Kennedy, "Stanford and the Schools," Stanford University (forthcoming). For additional listings see Education Week, July 27, 1983, pp. 43-44.
3. For useful critiques of some of the reports identified above see, for example, Lawrence C. Stedman and Marshall S. Smith, "Recent Reform Proposals for American Education, forthcoming in Contemporary Education

Review, Vol. 2, No. 2, 1983, and papers by Alan P. Wagner ("The National Reports: Financing Improvements in Educational Quality") and Frances Kemmerer ("The National Reports: Research and Recommendations") prepared at the Center for Educational Research and Policy Studies, SUNY-Albany.

4. See, for example, Chapter 2, "We Want It All."

5. For additional data see Tables 41 and 42 of the Feistritzer report, The Condition of Teaching, p. 73.

6. The heavy regulation of public education stands in curious contrast to a currently popular academic notion about educational institutions and systems borrowed from Karl Weick ("Educational Organizations as Loosely-Coupled Systems," Administrative Science Quarterly, Vol. 21, No. 1, 1976, pp. 1-19). At one level we understand ourselves to be "loosely coupled," but when one thinks about the total amount of external regulation that stands over and around every formal instructional setting in the public schools, the coupling is about as "loose" as a police officer's handcuffs!

7. See, for example, those advanced by Governor Thomas H. Kean of New Jersey (Education Week, September 14, 1983, pp. 1, 19), but not dissimilar proposals have also been advanced in Virginia and California.

Chapter One   Inquiry as the Organizing Principle
                     for Educational Reform in America

1. There is nothing new under the sun. There are others who have from time to time proposed similar ideas and to whose work I am indebted. Prominent among them are Robert J. Schaefer (The School as a Center of Inquiry, Harper & Row, Publishers, 1967) and Arthur Coladarci (Chapter 13, in George Kneller, editor, Foundations of Education, John Wiley, 1967). More recent work related to this concept may be found in numerous citations contained in Communication Quarterly published by The Institute for Research on Teaching at Michigan State University, especially Volume 6, Catalog, 1983-84.

2. "Client" is not the word I really want to use but I could not come up with another. See my later comments in Chapter Three.

3. I am indebted to John Nisbet at the University of Aberdeen, Scotland, for reminding me of John Dewey's concept of "warranted assertability," a term Dewey preferred to the more common "truth" because of his recognition that knowledge was always somewhat tentative. No matter how firmly grounded, empirical knowledge is always fallible. In the more than forty years intervening since Dewey addressed these matters, our understandings of the nature of behavioral and social inquiry (cf. Chapter Six) reinforce Dewey's sense of caution, especially as we are confronted by different epistemologies and the multiple perspectives forthcoming from the academic disciplines and professional specialties. See John Dewey, "Propositions, Warranted Assertability, and Truth," Journal of Philosophy, XXXVIII (1941).

4. This seems as good a place as any to insert a caveat. This essay attempts to address the formal institutions of learning and the frames of reference the professionals serving in those institutions carry with them as they undertake their responsibilities. Education and learning take place in

Introduction

other places and through other means; these other means are likely to be subject to tremendous growth and expansion, principally as a consequence of the satellite, television, video-recording, and computer revolution we are now entering. But there will still be schools, colleges, and universities, and exciting and innovative technologies now bursting upon us are still means to ends that must be orchestrated to satisfy society that at least the minimum common aims required and desired are fulfilled. That role will continue to be performed by institutionalized forms of schooling whose professionals, in any case, ought to be acting on the basis of the inquiry frame of mind proposed herein.

5. Cf. the studies published by Bruce Pesseau and Paul Orr, "The Outrageous Underfunding of Teacher Education," Phi Delta Kappan, Vol. 62, No. 2, October, 1980, p. 100.

Chapter Two   Problems in Supporting Education on the Processes and Products of Inquiry

1. N.L. Gage, The Scientific Basis of the Art of Teaching, Teachers College Press, 1978.

2. Robert R. Spillane, "Some Unfortunate Assumptions," Phi Delta Kappan, September, 1982, Vol. 64, No. 1, p. 21.

3. I am referring here to the brouhaha that arose over the early release of the data and conclusions of James Coleman's work he later published as Public and Private Schools.

4. This kind of judgment is epitomized in the comments of staff writers of NASULGC's the green sheet who ask: "When do we start to fund education research that has demonstrated its professionalism and productivity...?" (Circular letter No. 11, August 23, 1983, p. 2).

5. Harry Judge, American Graduate Schools of Education, Ford Foundation, 1982, p. 20.

Chapter Three   Projected Outcomes and Consequences

1. This notion is in league with Burton Blatt's dictum that it would be far better if universities could come to spend more time learning than knowing (Burton Blatt, In and Out of the University: Essays on Higher and Special Education, University Park Press, 1982, p. 61). It expresses the same notion of an identity between basic process and aim that ought especially to characterize our formal institutions of learning at all levels of the system.

2. David S. Seeley, Education Through Partnership: Mediating Structures and Education, Ballinger Publishing Company, 1981, p. 65. Neither sense of the term "client" adequately captures what we would mean, for, as Seeley points out, "the first disempowers students and their parents; the second disempowers teachers and professional staffs."

3. Such a proposal is sketched out in my "The Necessary Revolution in Teacher Education," Phi Delta Kappan, September, 1982, Vol. 64, No. 1, pp. 15-18. Related work by others includes B.O Smith, A Design for a School of Pedagogy, U.S. Government Printing Office, 1980, #E-80-42000; Goodlad's A Place Called School (especially Chapter 9); Lawrence A. Cremin, "The Educa-

tion of the Educating Profession," The Knowledge Base for the Preparation of Educational Personnel, Vol. 1, American Association for Colleges of Teacher Education, 1978; and Donna H. Kerr, "Teaching Competence and Teacher Education in the United States," Teachers College Record, Spring, 1983, Vol. 84, No. 3, pp. 525-552.

4. The most complete exposition of this formulation is to be found in A Design for a School of Pedagogy cited in footnote #3 immediately above.

5. A more detailed exposition of the liberal arts base for teacher education will be available in my revision of "The Necessary Revolution for Teacher Education" which will appear in a forthcoming yearbook of the National Society for the Study of Education edited by Charles Case and James Matthes.

Chapter Five   The Purposes of Educational Inquiry

1. Lee J. Cronbach and Patrick Suppes, editors, Research for Tomorrow's Schools: Disciplined Inquiry for Education, The Macmillan Company, 1969, pp. 20-21.

2. Three generic references, however, that are worth pursuing of, admittedly, many that might be identified are: Carol H. Weiss and Michael J. Bucuvalas, Social Science Research and Decision-Making, Columbia University Press, 1980; Carol H. Weiss, editor, Using Social Research in Public Policy Making, Lexington Books, 1977; and Charles E. Lindblom and David K. Cohen, Usable Knowledge: Social Science and Social Problem Solving, Yale University Press, 1979.

3. In recent years numerous publications of considerable usefulness have come out on evaluation. To mention just a few to lead those who are not familiar with the literature to "streams" from which they can then branch out, consider: Lee J. Cronbach and Associates, Toward Reform of Program Evaluation, Jossey-Bass, 1981; Lee J. Cronbach, Designing Evaluations of Educational and Social Programs, Jossey-Bass, 1982; William R. Meyers, The Evaluation Enterprise; A Realistic Appraisal of Evaluation Careers, Methods, and Applications, Jossey-Bass, 1981; and Egon S. Guba and Yvonne S. Lincoln, Effective Evaluation, Jossey-Bass, 1981.

4. Literature on educational development is difficult to come by. Its absence is itself symptomatic of the inattention to matters that ought to be of central concern to those interested in better utilizing the results of learning in instructional practice. See, however, John Hemphill annd F.S. Rosenau, editors, Educational Development: A New Discipline for Self-Renewal, Center for the Advanced Study of Education Administration, Monograph No. 24, 1973; John Hemphill, A Model for Educational Development," Programmatic Research and Development in Education: Position, Problems, Propositions, edited by Frank C. Pratzner and Jerry P. Walker, The Center for Vocational and Technical Education, The Ohio State University, 1972; and Richard E. Schutz, "The Conduct of Development in Education," Phi Delta Kappa Research Service Center, Occasional Paper No. 14, no date (circa 1973); and Richard E. Schutz, "The Nature of Educational Development," Journal of Research and Development in Education, 1970, No. 3, pp. 39-63.

Chapter Three

Chapter Six   Characteristics of Inquiry for Education

1. I have in another publication acknowledged my debt to John R. Seeley's "Social Science? Some Probative Problems," Sociology on Trial, edited by Stein and Vidach, Prentice Hall, 1963, in coming to terms with the characteristics of behavioral and social inquiry, but it seems appropriate to repeat it here.

2. Herbert W. Simons, "The Management of Metaphor," Rigor and Imagination: Essays from the Legacy of Gregory Bateson, C. Wilder-Mott and John H. Weakland, editors, Praeger, 1981, p. 135.

3. See Hendrik D. Gideonse, Robert Koff, and Joseph J. Schwab, editors, Values, Inquiry, and Education, CSE Monograph Series in Evaluation #9, Center for the Study of Evaluation, UCLA, 1980, for a more extensive treatment of this theme. Also cf. Richard Rudner, "The Scientist qua Scientist Makes Value Judgments," Philosophy of Science, Vol. 20, No. I, January, 1953, pp. 1-6.

4. In particular, Syracuse Univerity's Thomas Green.

5. For example, see Lee J. Cronbach, "Beyond the Two Disciplines of Scientific Psychology," American Psychologist, February, 1975.

6. "Illumination" is a concept that has also been applied to evaluation strategies as, for example, in the work of Malcolm Parlett (with Garry Deardon), Introduction to Illuminative Evaluation: Studies in Higher Education, Pacific Soundings Press, 1967) and that of Robert Stake.

7. One implication deserving mention can be found in the emergence in recent years of deliberate attempts to conduct research from the dual perspectives of practitioners and academics. So-called interactive research models or practitioner/researcher inquiry approaches are being experimented with in many places. Three examples are the work done by Beatrice A. Ward and William Tikunoff at the Far West Laboratory for Educational Research and Development, Ann Lieberman's efforts at Teachers College, Columbia University, and Susan Florio's work at Michigan State University. Arthur S. Bolster deals with the divergent perspectives of teachers and researchers concerning how knowledge is formulated and determined in "Toward a More Effective Model of Research on Teaching," Harvard Educational Review, Vol. 53, No. 3, August, 1983, pp. 294-308. Also, see Marilyn Rauth, Brenda Biles, Lovely Billups, and Susan Veitch, American Federation of Teachers Educational Research and Dissemination Program (NIE-G-81-0021) for an important prototype of teacher-initiated attempts to link to research in ways useful to their peers. Ann Lieberman, Beatrice Ward, and Lee Shulman serve on the advisory board for the project. See also David R. Olson, "The Languages of Instruction: The Literate Bias of Schooling," R.C. Anderson, R. Spiro, and W.E. Montigue, editors, Schooling and the Acquisition of Knowledge, Lawrence Erlbaum Associates, 1977, and Robert Yinger, "Learning the Language of Practice," presented at the conference "First Years of Teaching: What are the Pertinent Issues?," Research and Development Center for Teacher Education, The University of Texas at Austin, March 1983. Relevant Swedish analysis may be found in Gunnar Bergendal, Knowledge and Higher Education, National Board of Universities and Colleges, 1983.

Chapter Seven   How Can Inquiry Products and Processes
                     Come to Improve Education?

    1. Egon G. Guba and David L. Clark, "One Perspective On Change,"
SEC Newsletter, The Ohio State University, Vol. 1, No. 2, 1965, pp. 2-5.
    2. Consider "Federal Research and Development Programs: The Decision-
making Process," House Report No. 1664, U.S. Government Printing Office,
1964; Hendrik D. Gideonse, "Research, Development, and the Improvement of
Education," Science, Vol. 162, November 1, 1968; and Chalmers W. Sherwin
and Raymond S. Isenson, "Project Hindsight," Science, Vol. 156, June 23,
1967.
    3. Hendrik D. Gideonse, "Research and Development for Education: A
Market Model," The Oregon Studies: Research, Development, Diffusion,
Evaluation, Volume III, Conceptual Frameworks, Teaching Research, A Division
of the Oregon System of Higher Education, 1972, pp. 12-48.
    4. See Ward S. Mason and Norman J. Boyan, "Perspectives on Educa-
tional R&D Centers," Journal of Educational Research and Development, Vol.
1, No. 4; Robert Glaser, "Discussion: New Myths and Old Realities," Harvard
Educational Review, Vol. 38, No. 4, Fall, 1968; G. Raisbeck, et al., Manage-
ment Factors Affecting Research and Exploratory Development, A.D. Little,
1965; and Ronald G. Havelock and Mary C. Havelock, Training for Change
Agents: A Gudie to the Design of Training Programs in Education and Other
Fields, Institute for Social Research, 1973.
    5. Egon G. Guba and David L. Clark, The Configurational Perspective:
A New View of Educational Knowledge Production and Utilization, Council for
Educational Development and Research, 1974.
    6. David R. Krathwohl, "The Perceived Ineffectiveness of Educational
Research and Some Recommendations," Educational Psychologist, Vol. 11, No.
2, 1974.
    7. Paul Berman and Milbrey Wallin McLaughlin, Federal Programs in
Support of Educational Innovation, Rand Corporation, 1976-1980; Dale Mann,
"The Impact of IMPACT II," Teachers College Record, Vol. 84, No. 4,
Summer, 1983; and several of the chapters, especially those by Dale Mann,
Willis Hawley, and Milbrey Wallin McLaughlin, in Dale Mann, editor, Making
Change Happen?, Teachers College Press, 1978.

Memo One   Teachers and Principals

    1. This is a very simple sentence which stands for a very complex set
of tasks. Designing a new school wherein professional roles are defined to
encourage conduct of essential practice-oriented inquiry and all the functions
of which are designed to rest on what is known about teaching and learning
must be thought of on the same scale as building, say, prototype tanks for
the military or satellites for NASA. The scale of effort would entail, for
conceptual design, several millions of dollars for each model, and several
hundred of million for each prototype. Compared to the annual operating costs
of schools and lower division baccalaureate instruction, the sums mentioned
above are actually quite small. We are not used to thinking in such terms in
education; on the views advanced here, we must begin to do so.

Chapter Seven

2. Gary Sykes, Teacher Education and the Professional Project: An Account of Its Predicaments, NIE, mimeo, May 18, 1983. Indeed, one way to look at this essay is as an explicit attempt to contribute to education's "professional project."

Memo Two   Governors

1. Dan Balz, "State Governments Leading the Drive to Upgrade Education, The Washington Post, August 1, 1983, p. 1 and Neal R. Peirce, "A Teacher-Governor Leads the Way," The Cincinnati Post, August 18, 1983, p. 7A.
2. See Recommendation #4 of the Merit Pay Task Force Report prepared for the Committee on Education and Labor, House of Representatives, October, 1983, p. 7

Memo Three   Chief State School Officers

1. Available evidence, however, suggests that even more fundamental work needs to be done on practices followed in some of the States on the basis of which program apoprovals are granted. In some States, for instance, institutions are approved for teacher education which do not even enjoy accreditation from the appropriate regional accrediting body. In many others, serious questions exist in the minds of teacher educators about the extent to which extant standards are applied differentially for public and private institutions or large and small.
2. Terry Herndon as interviewed by Noel Epstein, The Washington Post, August 14, 1983, p. C3.
3. Evidence of this phenomenon can be found in the article by Phillip C. Schlechty and Victor S. Vance, "Institutional Responses to the Quality/Quantity Issue in Teacher Training," Phi Delta Kappan, Vol. 65, No. 2, October, 1983, pp. 94-101.
4. The year my own College of Education identified such additional requirements for admissions, the one-year fall-off in completion of applications was 42 percent! Even the least perceptive among us can translate that quickly into budgetary terms.

Memo Four   Heads of Teacher Education

1. B. Othanel Smith in collaboration with Stuart H. Silverman, Jean M. Borg, and Betty V. Fry, A Design for a School of Pedagogy, U.S. Government Printing Office, 1980, No. E-80-42000. Also, see my "The Necessary Revolution in Teacher Education, Phi Delta Kappan, Vol. 64, No. 1, pp. 15-18.
2. For a recent exposition of this point of view and a somewhat distressing set of responses see Richard Wisniewski, Too Many Schools of Education? Too Little Scholarship?, Society of Professors of Education Monograph Series 1983 and Ayers Bagley, editor, The Right Questions?: Six Reviews of Too Many Schools of Education, Too little Scholarship?, Society of Professors of Education Monograph Series, 1983.

Memo Five   <u>Director, National Institute of Education</u>

1. One of the most intriguing examples of this kind of effort was a study done thirteen years ago for the Ford Foundation by Robert J. Meeker and Daniel M. Weiler, <u>A New School for the Cities</u>, System Development Corporation, Santa Monica, CA, SP-369/000/02. The document is a final draft of a preliminary design for a new urban school. To call it imaginative would be understating the case. What is needed is a variety of alternative conceptualizations, a judicious selection of a half dozen and then the systematic development of full scale working models, an effort which would dwarf current or past R&D efforts in education but would still probably cost no more, as I have already suggested, than the development projects associated with individual weapons systems in the military or specialized satellites in NASA.

2. One could argue that the nature of the objections raised to MACOS constitute the single most powerful argument for the need for such a curriculum on the American educational scene! Whatever one's views on the merits, however, professional educators as a whole cannot be said to have covered themselves with glory in their willingness to give way before narrow sectarian interests, either as to curricular content or process. Making such statements should not be interpreted as a defense of any and everything that was done in using MACOS materials; on the other hand, for NIE to follow a policy whose effect is to deny teachers, schools, and pupils of all ages the benefits of fully-developed curricular materials over such misplaced anxieties is, at the very least, an outstanding anomaly given NIE's overall charge.

3. A first such study was my <u>Educational Research and Development in the United States</u> completed in connection with the 1969 OECD policy review. Additional examples of such work include: Stacy Churchill, <u>Modeling a National Educational R&D System: A Conceptual Framework</u>, Ontario Institute for Studies in Education, 1974; William Paisley and Associates, <u>The Status of Educational Research and Development in the United States</u>, NIE, 1975; Michael Radnor, Durward Hofler, and Harriet Spivak, <u>Agency/Field Relationships in the Educational R/D&I System: A Policy Analysis for the National Institute of Education</u>, 1976, and <u>Regionalism in Educational R/D&I</u>, 1977, and <u>Strengthening Fundamental Research Relevant to Education</u>, 1977, and, with Earl C. Young and Raymond J. Buckley, <u>Comparative Research, Development and Innovation: With Implications for Education</u>, 1977, The Center for Interdisciplinary Study of Science and Technology, Northwestern University; and O. W. Markley, Principal Investigator, <u>The Normative Structure of Knowledge Production and Utilization in Education</u>, EPRC 3555-13, Educational Policy Research Center, Stanford Research Institute, 1975. The work of Burkart Holzner and his associates at the University of Pittsburgh should also be noted.

4. The selective thrust of this recommendation will be controversial. Smaller programs have -- and almost certainly will again -- respond by saying that the big are out to sink the small. The quantitative character of the argument advanced invites the reaction. In the context of the proposals advanced in this essay, such reactions are red herrings. First, next to no teacher education programs look like the ones being recommended. Second,

Memo Five

that means that large and small alike will have to justify themselves in terms of their specifics, both as to curricular content and requisite expertise. The problem with the objection, however, is that once the knowledge base and underlying expertise required for offering teacher education programs are specified, it will be all too obvious that a small number of faculty will not be able to fulfill the requirements. The upshot is that size is necessary but not sufficient. Connection to inquiry and knowledge is necessary but not sufficient. The proof of the pudding will be the worth of the total configuration. In any case, omelets cannot be made without cracking eggs!

5. As final editing was being completed, a copy of the recommendations being considered by the National Council on Educational Research crossed my desk (Kendall O. Price, An Executive Summary: Policy Recommendations for Managing the National Institute of Education's Regional Educational Laboratories, The Sequoia Institute, October 17, 1983). Time was insufficient to complete a thorough review of the proposals contained therein but at least one serious anomaly emerged in the form of the recommendation that fully eight of the twelve recommended R&D Center foci for the upcoming (and now delayed for one year) Lab/Center competition be oriented to designated subject matter areas of the school curriculum. The anomaly is two-fold. First, if the centers are to represent the major thrust of NIE's basic research endeavors, then focusing on curricular areas is likely to give an applied cast which will make basic research more difficult to justify. Second and more serious is the contradiction to be found in organizing research centers around curricular areas in light of NIE's standing prohibition against curriculum development. High tolerance for ambiguity may characterize academia generally, but it can be carried too far! The recommendations being considered by NCER are far-ranging and must be subjected to more thorough and thoughtful consideration by the research community and various representatives of the educational policy community before adoption by the Council.

Memo Six   Executive Director, NCATE

1. I gratefully acknowledge the help of Willis Hawley, Dean of George Peabody College for Teachers, Vanderbilt University, on a currently dormant project to assist ourselves and our colleagues in stimulating attention to inquiry processes. The notes of our conversations together made the drafting of this initial listing much easier.

2. Cf., again, the work on interactive research models by Tikunoff and Ward, Lieberman, and Florio mentioned in footnote #7, Chapter Six.

Memo Seven   Research and Development Community

1. This is vital for practitioners, too, who ought to be acting on the basis of knowledge derived from inquiry and who must, therefore, be aware of this important parameter of what it means "to know" in the behavioral and social domain.

2. One thinks, for example, of the current controversies over the relative performance of public and private schools, the effective schools research, the importance of principal leadership, or time on task as illustra-

tions of instances where less than optimal sensitivity to the "injured foot phenomenon" has been displayed by one or more of the published protagonists.

Memo Ten   Education Writers in the Popular Press

1. Kenneth M. Pierce, "Summer with Homer and Vergil," TIME, August 15, 1983, p. 39.
2. Haynes Johnson, "Merit," The Washington Post, June 19, 1983, p. A3.
3. "Secretary Bell Would Fund 'Master-Teacher' Projects," Education Week, July 27, 1983, p. 13.
4. Rev. Celsus Griese, O.F.M., The Cincinnati Enquirer, August 25, 1983, p. A-15.
5. Associated Press, "Survey Finds Caliber of Students Drawn to Teaching on Decline," The Cincinnati Enquirer, August 25, 1983, p. B-20. The impression created is clearly negative; it is significant, however, that the report from which the AP story was written contains the following explicit caution on the findings respecting extended programs: "It is not clear whether this lack of support represents the perception that such a reform is undesirable, infeasible, or both" (National Center for Education Statistics Bulletin NCES 83-225b, "Survey of Teacher Education: Perceptions of Methods of Improvement," p. 2).
6. Additional evidence of this may be found in the Schlechty and Vance article cited in footnote #3, Memo Three.
7. The TIME article cited in footnote #1 above is one example. Another is the article by Timothy Foote, "NEH Chief: Tough Talk on Teaching," The Washington Post Fall Education Review, August 7, 1983, pp. 1, 8-12, 19.

Memo Eleven   College and University Presidents

1. A blatant example of the existence of unwarranted status hierarchies if not outright prejudice can be seen in the gathering held several months ago at Yale University to discuss "'the crisis of quality' within the nation's teaching profession" (Sheppard Ranbom, "Educators Seek Solutions to 'Crisis' in Teaching," Education Week, March 2, 1983, pp. 1,16). Not a single head of a school or college of education was invited to the meeting. That a similar gathering to address a perceived "crisis" in medical, legal, or engineering education could have been convened without at least a representative sampling of the appropriate deans being present is simply inconceivable. As an indicator of interest where there has been precious little, many teacher educators felt gratified over the attention. On the other hand, there were subtle messages of a more negative cast which many found disconcerting and sobering. Those responsible for or interested in educational reform need to think seriously why such events can happen and what it means for the prospects for and routes to substantial improvement.
2. At one institution, for example, only a few years ago, a graduate dean raised challenging questions about his institution's commitment to teacher education. In his view the necessary relationship with the State Department of Education represented an unwarranted intrusion into legitimate faculty

Memo Seven

prerogatives and responsibilities for curriculum definition as a consequence of the need to conform to certification standards and to be subjected to evaluation by that agency for purposes of program approval.

3. Some renewed hope that greater attention will be paid to the relationships between universities and the schools is to be found in the holding of a recent meeting of six university presidents and four education deans at Pajaro Dunes, California. A far broader representation will be required, however, in the long run; only two of the six presidents were from public institutions and one of those was just about to recommend a forty percent cut in his institution's School of Education, and of the four deans represented, but one was from a public institution. Still, the example may prove to be a useful stimulus, and the caution and reserve expressed in the press release flowing from the meeting certainly indicated that those assembled understood the difficulty, complexity, and delicacy of the tasks they had convened to discuss. ("University, School Links Urged" and "The Role of Colleges in School Improvement," Education Week, August 24, 1983, pp. 1, 17.)

4. That there is room for considerable instructional improvement in higher education generally is evident from some of the back-up studies done for the National Commission on Excellence in Education, studies which, rather surprisingly, did not seem to figure much in the Commission's heralded report. Among those studies are reports which indicate that the test score declines shown for lower education are neither reversed by what happens in college nor are they held constant. In fact, the decline in teaching quality, if that is what we are looking at, also afflicts higher education. This omission is suggestive in terms of the possibility of selective attention on the part of the public and the policy community. One might well ask, in a parallel vein, why, given the orientation-to-the-economy-and-international-trade-competition basis for at least three of the major reports, there has not been at least as much attention to the quality of the students going to business schools whose scores are even lower than those of prospective teachers! In the answer to that question, one suspects, lies further evidence of the scapegoating phenomenon which at least partially explains the exclusivity of focus accorded teacher quality and teacher preparation programs.

Memo Twelve   Executive Director, AERA

1. Many of the ideas contained in this and the memo to the Executive Director of AACTE grow out of a stimulating collaborative effort with Dean Robert Koff, School of Education, SUNY-Albany following on the work of the Salishan Deans. Ideas here are liberally pirated from the paper we jointly authored for the 1982 Annual Meeting of AERA in New York under the title "Inquiry, Scholarship, and Teacher Education: Issues and Implications."

2. Several readers of drafts of this essay speculated on the transportability of its themes beyond the borders of the United States. Clearly, the specifics of the memos to which this is a footnote would be almost wholly inapplicable. I would argue, however, that insofar as the analysis has accurately described the purposes, characteristics, and uses of inquiry in support of educational practice, it has applicability elsewhere in the world, although the full extent of that applicability would certainly depend on

resources, supporting technology, and the willingness to champion levels of
professional preparation requisite to the operation of an educational system as
projected herein.

Memo Thirteen   Executive Director, AACTE

1. As this manuscript was undergoing final editing still a new potential
competing influence emerged. Seventeen institutions of higher education met
in mid-October to discuss joining forces to improve the preparation of teachers
in the Nation's schools by attracting better qualified students and taking the
steps needed to make teaching a learned profession. While no specific recommendations or organizational steps were taken at the October 11-13 meeting at
Racine, Wisconsin, those attending did agree to reconvene in the Spring of
1984 to continue their discussions.
Last March Harry Judge shared his impression that teacher education
institutions in America seemed bent on identifyingtheir own unique characteristics and, then, on the basis of those characteristics, rapidly seeking to
distance ourselves from one another. It was a characterization with the ring of
truth; if so, we may be in serious trouble. The answer cannot be lowest
common denominator. When the standards of excellence are identified to which
teacher education must aspire if it is to be an **instrument** of reform rather
than its **object**, they will emerge from reflective scholarship and the commitment to the developing knowledge base.
2. The wrestling match whether to include this footnote was closely
fought. I have been struck by a characteristic of conflict within teacher
education which, I believe, gets in the way of teacher educators making more
substantial contributions to policy dialog and generalized reform efforts. That
characteristic is a tendency to personalize our conflicts with one another. It
is not necesssary to describe it in detail. Mentioning it publicly in this way
may be sufficient to lead us all to attend to its diminution.

Chapter Nine   Reprise, Counter Arguments, and Promise

1. David Seeley argues this case, for example, in his book Education
Through Partnership: Mediating Structures and Education, Ballinger Publishing
Company, 1981, especially Chapter 5, "Pathological Professionalism." The
characterization of knowledge developed in this essay, however, is dramatically
different from the one he describes.
2. Two examples that can be cited are Arthur G. Powell, The Uncertain
Profession - Harvard and the Search for Educational Authority, Harvard
University Press, 1980, especially Chapter 9, "The Lure of Social Science" and
Alan R. Tom, "The Reform of Teacher Education through Research: A Futile
Quest," Teachers College Record, Vol. 82, No. 1, Fall, 1980, pp. 15-30.
3. These are sentiments attributed to William J. Bennett by Timothy
Foote in "NEH Chief: Tough Talk on Teaching," The Washington Post Fall
Education Review, August 7, 1983, pp. 1,8. The out-of-hand rejection of
pedagogy was equally baldly expressed by Mortimer Adler November 4, 1983, in
Milwaukee at the meeting of the American Educational Studies Association.

Chapter Nine

ORDER FORM

DETACH AND MAIL

ORDER FORM

Number of copies _____ @$5.95 each   Total _____

Reduced price for over five copies:

Number of copies _____ @$4.00 each   Total _____

                      Postage and Handling _____ $ .75

                              Total Remittance _____

Mail COPIES to: Mail ORDER to:

_____   Louis Fisher ML#2
_____   College of Education
_____   University of Cincinnati
_____   Cincinnati, Ohio 45221